SELF-PORTRAIT
of a
TEXAS COWBOY
—ASS OVER TEAKETTLE—

Stories told and Illustrated by

Brian Larremore

and

Written by Jean Larremore

authorHOUSE®

AuthorHouse™
1663 Liberty Drive
Bloomington, IN 47403
www.authorhouse.com
Phone: 1-800-839-8640

First published by AuthorHouse   02/18/2012

ISBN: 978-1-4685-5352-9 (sc)
ISBN: 978-1-4685-5351-2 (hc)
ISBN: 978-1-4685-5346-8 (ebk)

Library of Congress Control Number: 2012902999

Printed in the United States of America

Dedicated in memory of my daughter, Leanna

And to my son, Jim,

Grandchildren, Justin, Bailey, and Cole

This is the way I remember it.

This Land We Love

Where wavy lines of heat abound,
Where lizard, cactus, and snakes are found,
Where horse and mule reluctantly go,
Where hell is only one foot below.

It's beauty is found by only few,
Where sky displays a different hue,
It's dangers are a daily given,
Where love of life and mind are driven.

Where life becomes a precious thing,
Where silence and peace of mind can ring,
Where stars at night ripen the sky above,
And life goes on, in this land we love.

Jean Larremore

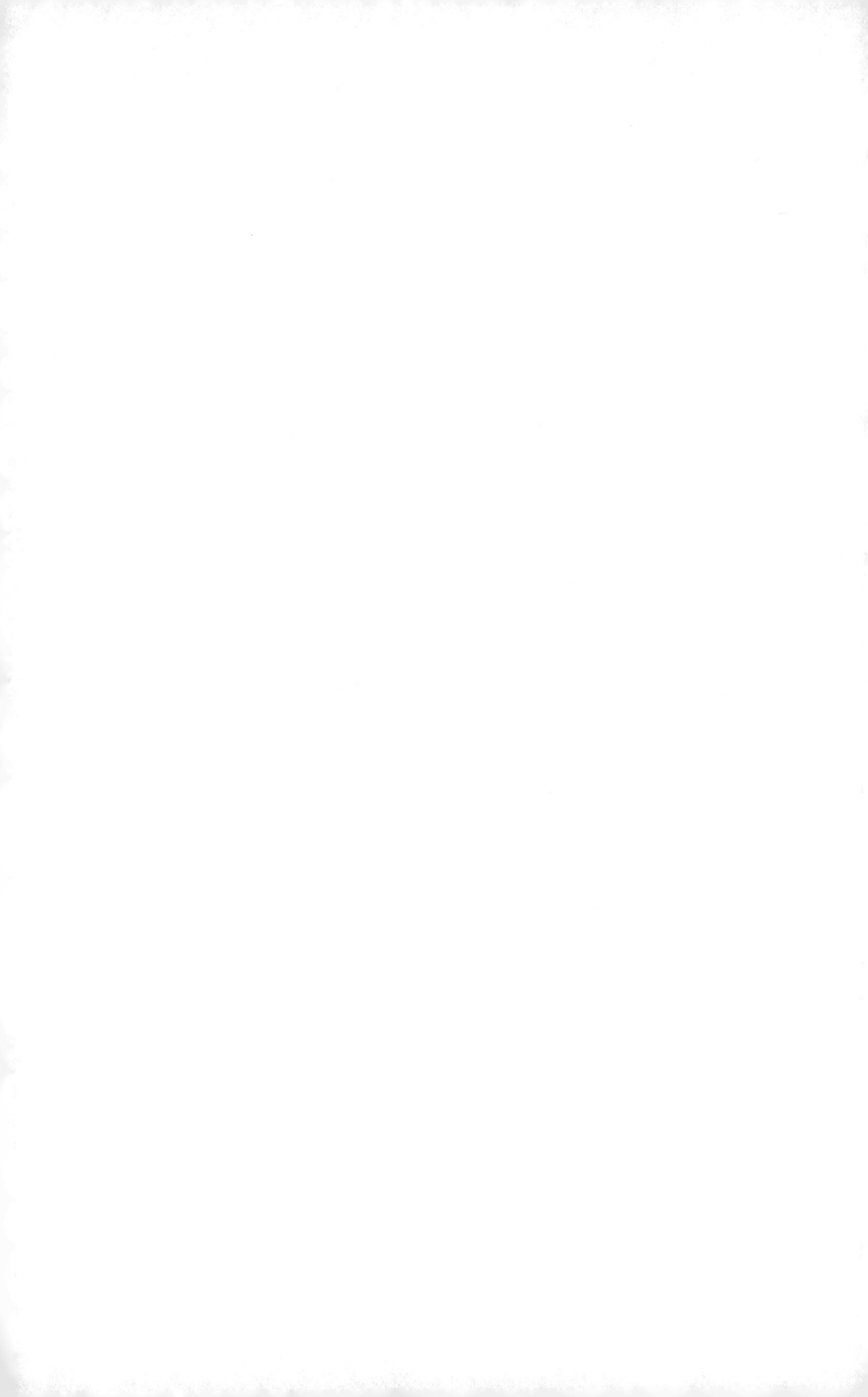

THE COWBOY

In days gone by, before there were cars, planes, trains, and technology, there lived a group of men known as the cowboy. These men fought to keep what was theirs, fought to keep life and limb, and fought for what they believed in. They were a people who believed that a man's word was his bond and truth was in the handshake shared. They fought and died for those beliefs. These hard working, trustworthy people are few and far between today, but every now and then, you may just be lucky enough to find one. I just happen to be one of those lucky few who married one.

BRIAN—THE 21ST CENTURY COWBOY

Brian was born in 1945 in Llano, Texas. His father, Wilma, and mother Lucille Larremore taught Brian responsibility at an early age. He grew up on horseback, on a pig farm, chasing coons up trees, fighting his brothers, and looking after his sister. Although he had a hard childhood, he never complained. He felt then, as he still feels, that his childhood taught him how to survive (especially being the youngest of 5 brothers!) and make the most of bad situations. His Mother and Father instilled in him a sense of respect for his elders, a sense of honesty to his fellow man, and the sense of being a true gentleman to the fairer sex. They also taught him to follow the motto set by the cowboys of old, that your word is your bond, and your handshake is as good as your word. He started college at Sul Ross in Alpine in 1965, got a degree in English, and went back later to get his Police Officer's license in 1986.

Brian was a Police Officer for 21 years at Sul Ross State University in Alpine, Texas, and was a Deputy Sheriff for 3 years in Brewster County. He retired in January of 2012 and has gone back to his first love . . . ranching. He has always said that "he worked to support his bad habit of ranching." He has raised the Texas State Dog, the Blue Lacy, most of his life and talks about and depicts some of his favorite dogs in these drawings. His Father, Wilma, also raised these dogs long before they became known as the Texas State Dog in 2005. Brian is known to always wear a black cowboy hat and has a Swisher Sweet cigarette hanging from his mouth most of the time. In the days of the old west, there may have been some "bad guys" who wore black hats, but Brian dispels that adage and many of his friends and family say that "guys who wear black hats aren't always bad."

Brian's parents taught him to admire beauty and the value of putting his thoughts and ideas to paper. In Brian's world, art says it all. He whittles, paints, and sketches and claims he is not a good artist, but being a little prejudice, I see true characterization and representation in his creative pieces and have felt for many years that I should share his talents. He has a very serious side to his art, but more often than not, his humor is what makes his art unique. The words that describe the pictures are Brian's and yes,

Texans do still talk this way. He has a low, slow Texas drawl that is a true depiction of the old west. To me, he is the epitome of a true west Texas cowboy. It just happens to be in the 21st century.

Brian married Ann Anderson in 1967 and was divorced in 1995. Ann's parents, Tinny and Luther Anderson had a little place south of Alpine that later became known as the Larremore-Anderson Ranch. Brian and Ann had two children, Leanna and Jim. Brian stayed on the Larremore-Anderson Ranch until 2000 when the owners of the land around the Larremore-Anderson asked if he would trade his land for some other land or buy him out. He decided to trade that country for some other country about 15 miles further south. Although the story is long and drawn out, over the last several years, Brain and I have fought hard against the ranch who are neighbors and who are attempting to take away our livelihood, our dream, his ranch. It is similar to the old west days of the land barons taking over little ranches any way they could. This rival ranch is very large, very prestigious, and very influential in today's society and is a corporation. Because we do not have much money and live pretty much hand-to-mouth, they know we are vulnerable. But as in old, a person should fight for what you believe in and fight for what is yours. The rival ranch has made claims that they are richer then God, have more money, more power, and more attorneys and will take everything from us if we continue the fight to keep our land. In an attempt to stay level-headed, Brian takes time to put into art form his memories, dreams, and humor. This book is a culmination of some of his artwork and the stories that go with the pieces. This artwork represents some of the trials, tribulations, wrecks, and humor that has occurred throughout the years We both love this land that we have, and the thought that someone would take it from us is painful, and what is more disturbing is that they are trying to take if from our children and our grandchildren.

Leanna passed away at the age of 17 and some of her story will come later in the book. Jim's story will come later in the book as well. Brian re-married in 2001, to me, Jean Raines.

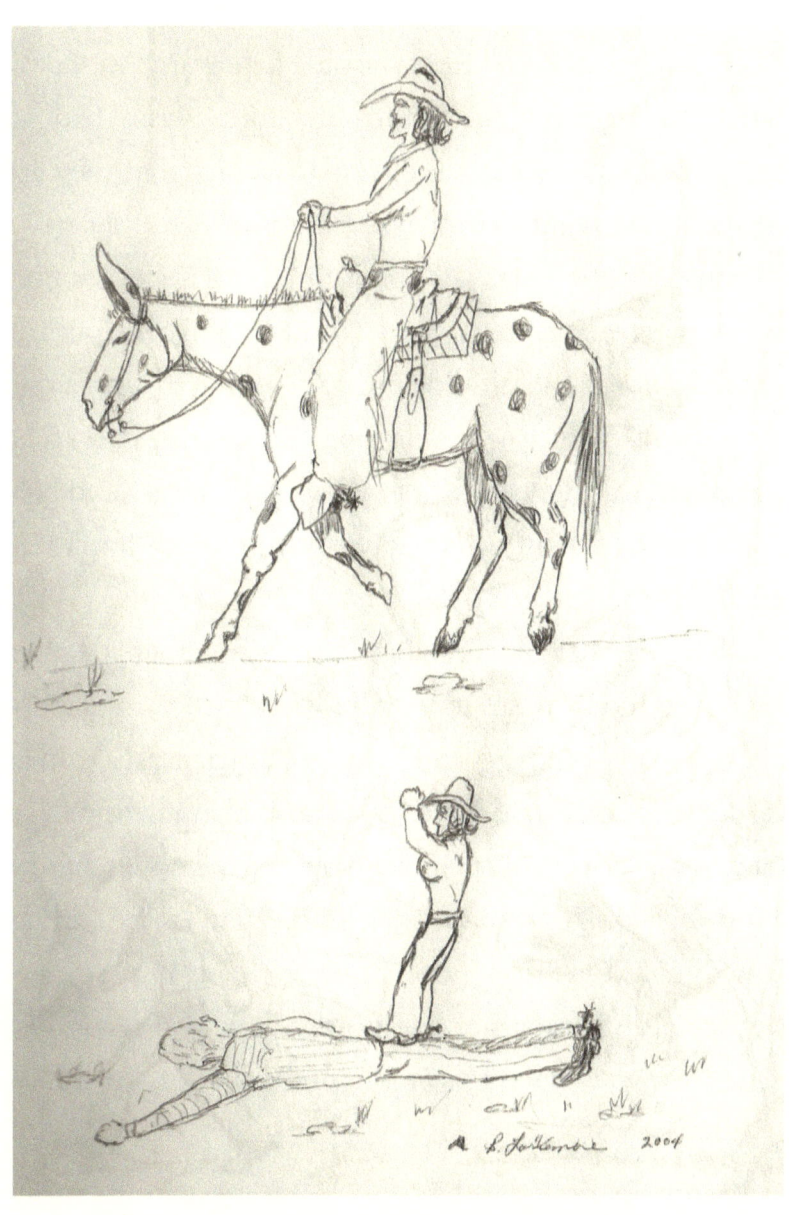

The day Jean and I got married

Brian and I got married on a November day and we had plans to move the cattle from the old Larremore-Anderson Ranch to the new ranch further south. Brian had an Appaloosa Mule at the time and Brian says that they are very rare. The mule's name was Blue and he could carry a man that weighed over 200 pounds and could pull a cow real easy. The day Brian and I got married Brian put me on ol' Blue and had me ride out to find a stray cow. Brian drew this picture for me on our fifth anniversary. The caption on this picture is "I let you get on my ass and kick it around the pasture the day we got married, don't you think it's time you got off?"

There are several drawbacks to being married to a cowboy. Among them is tripping over things underfoot in the house or garage such as saddles, harnesses, ropes, hay, feed, spurs, branding irons, or any other ranch related item you might think of. Also, you never know what he will bring into the house after a hard day in the saddle. Cow dung, horse dung, dog dung. etc., etc, etc. You get the picture. My daughter-in-law, Mandy, and sister-in-law, Jeanne, or any other cowboy's wife can attest to this as well. But then again, it's the life we've chosen and love; as well as we love our cowboys.

Some of the stories told by Brian are illustrated and other illustrations are what Brian would call doodling and draws just for the fun of it.

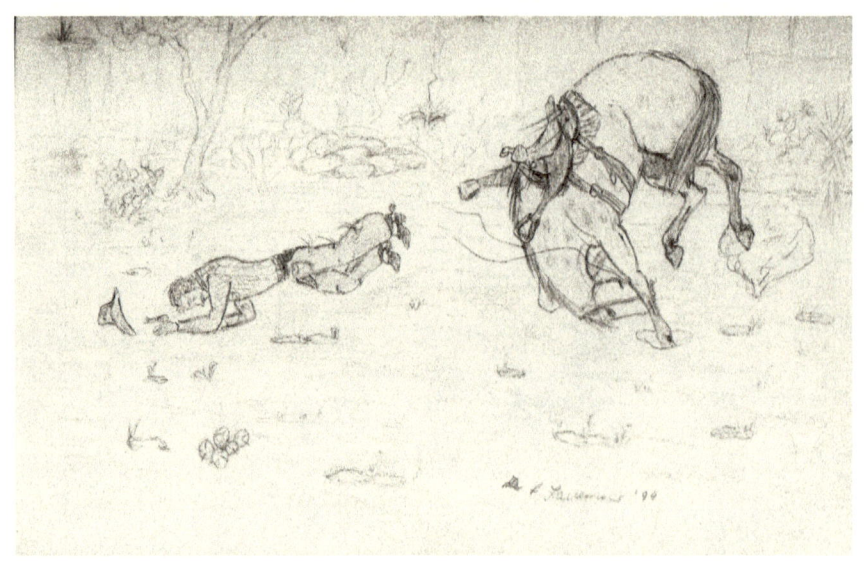

Sugar and the badger hole

BUTT BUSTER—ASS OVER TEAKETTLE

I married my first wife, Ann Anderson, when I was 22 years old. Ann's father, Luther, and I were pretty good friends and they had a small ranch about 20 miles south of Alpine, Texas. That was some rough ol' country. It's mostly rocks, mountains, canyons, cactus, and any other plant that will stick and stab you or kill your cattle or horses. It's part of the Chihuahua Desert but, I loved every inch of it and every minute of being there and liked nothin' better than to be in the saddle riding that country. However, some of the wrecks I had on that place were bloody and bone crushing, but I wouldn't have traded it for the world.

One day I was on a young mare, Sugar, and we had to go to the top of the mountain to gather some bulls and put them out in the pasture with the cows. Some of those bulls were pretty mean and would hook the horse if they could. As I was trying to push the bulls out of a canyon, I had to get around them in a hurry so they wouldn't hook my horse. We hit a dead run to get around them and my mare and I both were watching the bulls and never saw the badger hole that Sugar stepped in. I only had time to kick loose from my stirrups when she flipped ass over teakettle and threw me out far enough where her rear end landed on my rear end. It knocked the wind out of me and blurred my vision and I just knew my pelvis was broken. I couldn't tell the black bulls from the cedar trees, but I could see that grey mare. I eased up to her and she was shaking like a leaf, but she let me get on her. I couldn't sit down on the saddle cause my rear was hurting so bad and had to ride mostly on my arms by pushing on the swells of my saddle. I rode up the canyon up to a water hole so I could wash my face to clear my vision and we started for home about a mile away. My mother-in-law, Tinny, was coming through the gate at my house and she got out of her car to shut the gate. She asked what was the matter with me, to which I replied "I've got a cracked ass," and she laughed, slapped her thigh, jumped in her car and drove off. I rode on up to the barn and her house and started to unsaddle Sugar. I figured she took care of me in that canyon; I was going to take care of her. Tinny was unloading groceries and noticed I was hobbling around and again asked if something was the matter. I told her "before you run off again, this mare rolled with me and

I think I've got a cracked ass!" She and my wife, Ann, drove me to the hospital where they ex-rayed me and told me nothing was broken. My tailbone may not have been broken, but it was sure bent, 'cause ever since then, it points west when I'm looking north.

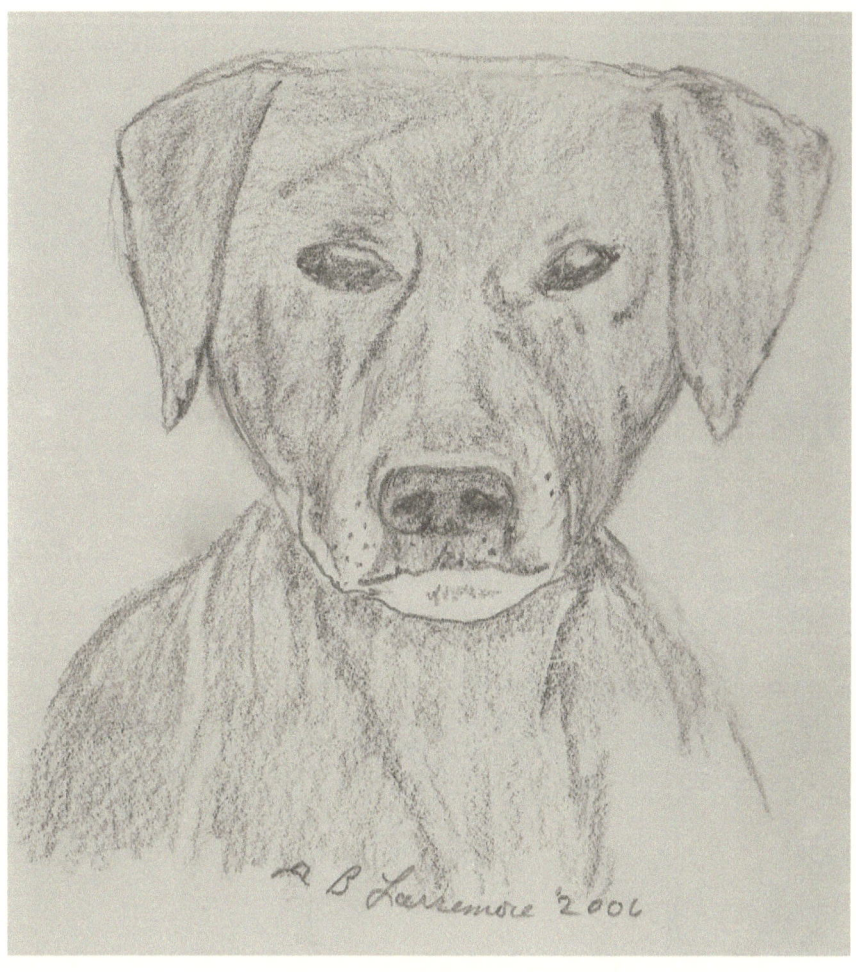

Wilkes, Texas Blue Lacy

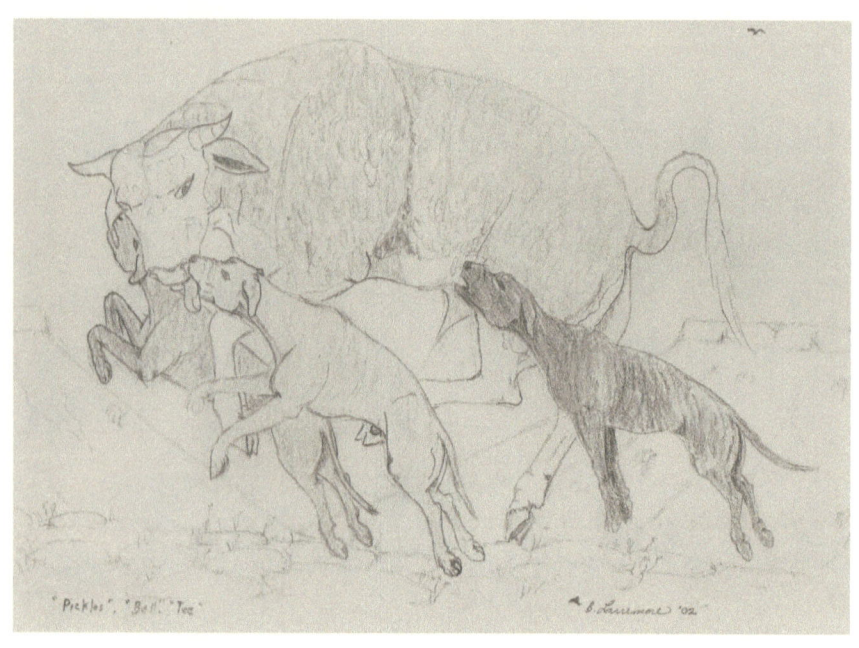

Pickles, Bell and Tee, Texas Blue Lacy Dogs

Best friends

"I've had a number of dogs over the years and each one of them had their own little quirks that made them unique. There was Wilkes, Bo, Sparky, Dee, Bell, Tee, and so many others. All top notch good dogs. Pickles was one of my half Lacy, half Leopard dogs I'd raised from one of my litters. These dogs are working fools. They love what they do and will do anything for you if you let em' work. One day, we had a bunch of cattle in pens having to cut down a long alley about 150' and around a corner. My son, Jim, who was about 19 at the time, and another ol' boy, who was pretty sorry and wouldn't or couldn't work the alley way where the cattle were sorted were with me. Jim had to work the gate by himself. I'd cut the cattle out and have to run them about 150 feet every time 'cause this ol' boy wouldn't move 15 feet. That dog Pickles kept wanting to work and I kept hollering for him to get back. When I started getting tired a light went on in my head and I decided "why not let him work and use him?" I'd cut out something and let him run it all the way down and I'd call him back and we'd repeat the process. I told that ol' sorry boy just to get out of the pens. We cut about 300 head of cattle that way. It's kinda pathetic when a dog can do a job a man is too lazy to do.

Another story about Pickles is one time when I'd missed a red Beef Master bull one day when I'd gathered my bulls. That bull was a little hot tempered. Apache Adams had a colt he needed to ride so he and Jim went after the bull. One of them was riding a colt and the other was riding a barefooted horse. The bull had brushed up in some cedar trees and the way they were mounted, they didn't think it would be too wise to rope that bull out of the cedar trees. My next day off I went horseback and took Pickles and my father-in-law, Luther, took an old 1945 Dodge weapons carrier. Luther told me he didn't think me and that dog could gather that bull. Pickles would get the bull started and I'd call Pickles back and the bull would go to traveling pretty good and Luther would cut in front of us with his power wagon. The bull would stop. We got the bull started 15 or 20 times. We finally got the bull out of the mountains down on the flat and the bull finally sulled up and wouldn't start again. Each time the bull would stop, Luther would ask "you want me to shotgun 'em?" When the bull wouldn't start the last time I told Luther to go ahead and get after him with the shotgun. After he'd shot-gunned him, Luther said "I told you couldn't gather him with just you and that dog!" It didn't hurt that old bull none, just made him mad, but I lost about 15 cents a pound because of the shotgun pellets in his hide and Luther trying to prove a point

Some of the best friends I've ever had were dogs. There were times that I wouldn't have been able to round up the cows without them. There are a number of times that I have to go up on top of Kokernot Mesa, which is part of our ranch. It's about 600 feet off the valley floor and the trail up to the top can kill you if you're not careful. My dogs go with me, just so they can work. It's bred into them and they love the challenge and I have to keep telling them "back" so they won't work when I don't need them to. They stop the herd by circling them and holding them up in one place till I can catch up and move the herd forward. I just call the dogs back and they come back and travel by me till I send them after a stray or a cow that doesn't want to stay in the herd. I have a signal with voice and hand to let the dogs know what I want.

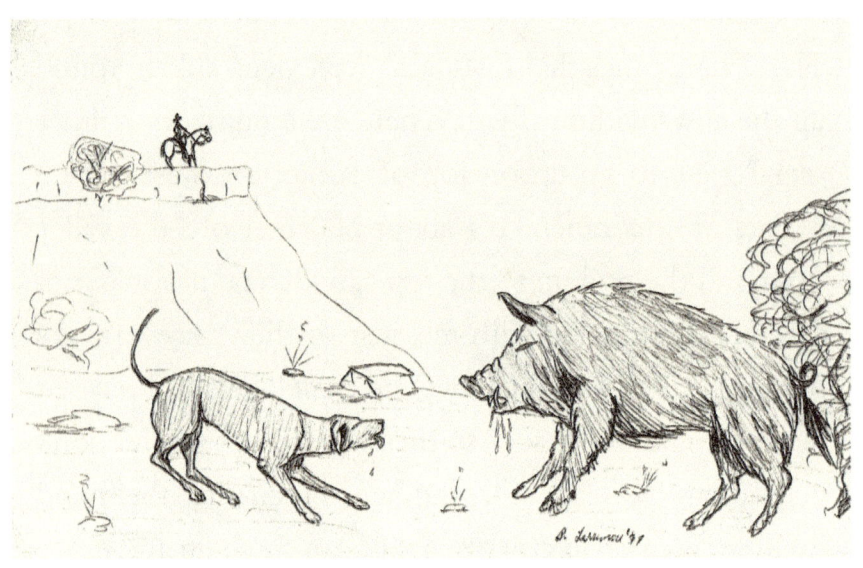

Bell, a Texas Blue Lacy and a wild hog

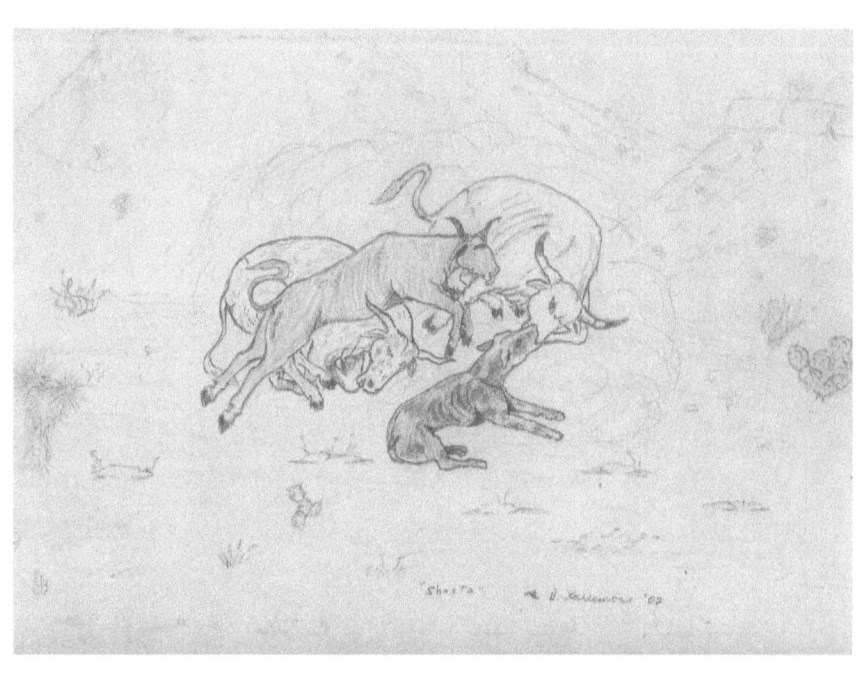

Shasta, Leopard dog

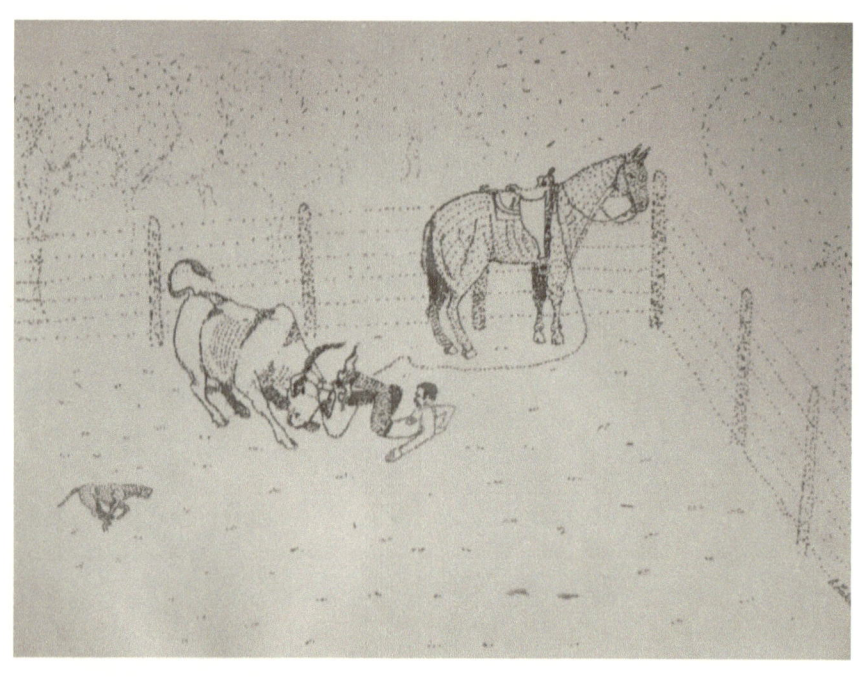

My father, Wilma and Freckles, a Leopard and Blue Lacy
mix

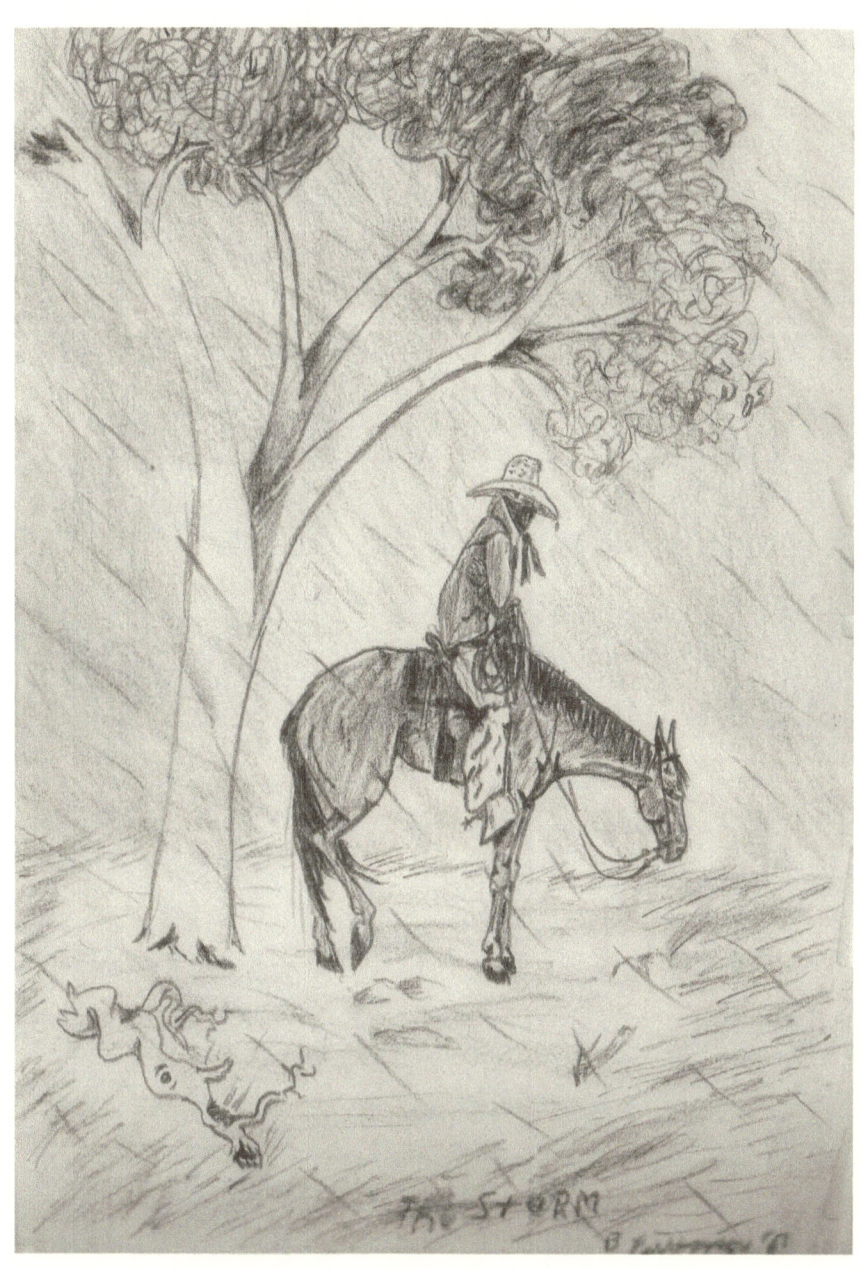

The Storm

COLD MORNING

I've lived through a number of really cold days in the saddle, but one day in particular that will stay with me was when I was working at a sheep and cattle ranch up in New Mexico that was one of the coldest places I've ever been or ever want to be. One morning me and some hands were going to move some sheep. It was a bitter, cold morning with about a foot of snow on the ground. None of us was looking forward to the job. It was starting to snow again and the wind was starting to blow. We all had our horses saddled and were ready to go and one of the hands, Jeff, only had on a football jacket which isn't made for 5 degree weather and snow blowing in at forty-five miles an hour. He started to get in the pickup and I asked him if he didn't want to get a heavier coat. He informed me right quick that he had been raised in that country, was young and rough, and that he could handle just about anything that old man winter could throw at him. I shut up, got in the pickup and went to get on the horses so we could gather the sheep. I had a rag tied over my ears with one of those wooly Russian caps tied over that, had on long johns, two pair of pants, two wool shirts, insulated coveralls, a hooded parka with nothing but a peep hole that I could look out of. I had on two pairs of wool socks, a pair of heavy boots and a pair of rubber over boots over those. I don't like the cold. It gets below 70 and I start looking for the second pair of socks and another jacket. I was riding a big horse named Pump Jack and he just needed to pack me and my clothes. That was one ugly horse. He had a really long head, too long for his body' and looked just like the horse's head on a pump jack. Every time he took a step, it looked like his head was going to lift his rear off the ground.

We worked those sheep for about four hours and started to push them though the gate. I noticed that, Jeff, who usually jumps down and opens the gates before I could, wasn't jumping off his horse too quick. He wasn't hassling his old pony and aggravating him like he usually did either. As a matter of fact, I noticed that Jeff's horse was doing most of the work and Jeff was just sitting up on top with both arms wrapped round himself. We shut the gate and hightailed it to the trucks. When we got there we all jumped off and started loading the horses in the trailers; that is all but Jeff. He just sat there on his horse looking around. I asked him what the holdup was and he looked back at me and finally answered that he didn't rightly figure he could get off that horse by himself. I figure he was right, cause his britches were about half frozen to the saddle and he was so cold he couldn't move much. We helped him off his horse, got him and the horse loaded up and started warming Jeff real slow with the truck heater. We finally got Jeff thawed out a little about the time we got home. I never did hear him say how much he could handle old man winter after that. He wore a big abundance of clothes after that too, just like the rest of us bunch of sissies.

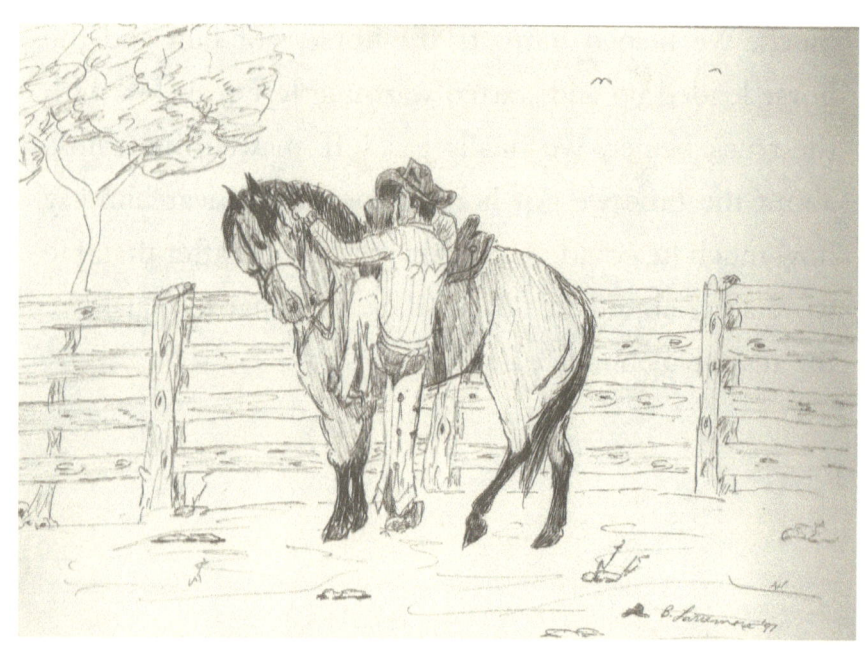

Bigun, Getting ready for the ride

The Day of the Wrecks

Roddy Schoenfeldt was a ranch foreman on some country out at the Elephant Mountain Ranch south of Alpine. One day he asked Don Coleman, Sam Dove and myself to help gather his personal cattle as the owner of the ranch told him to get rid of them. Now those old cows were mountain Hereford cattle that had been given to Roddy because they were more trouble to gather than the former lessor of the ranch, Ted Gray, thought they were worth. I had helped gather some of those old cows the first few times that they had been gathered, and I knew gathering them again was going to be a chore.

Roddy had the cows running in the lower Calamity Creek pasture, half of which was head high in mesquite and white brush so thick that you couldn't ride through unless you were on a horse that was about half the size of a javalina hog. The other side of the creek had been root plowed and was plumb full of holes. Looked like a gopher town. You took your life in your own hands every time you hit a lope cause your horse couldn't see those holes and would be upside down with you faster than you could spit. I'd had three bad spills in that rotten ground.

Roddy lined us up through the pasture on the root plowed side of the creek to see if we couldn't find the cattle on the open side. Sam Dove was riding a knot-headed bay horse that somebody had more than half spoiled. Roddy was riding a yellow roping horse that belonged to somebody else, and Don was riding a brown horse that would carry you through the pasture if you didn't want to get a whole lot done. I was riding a horse I called Bigun. He was a sorrel blaze face with a left back stocking. He stood about 16 hands high and was one of the best horses that I ever rode after you got the edge off him. Of course by the time you did that, he generally looked like a gutted snow bird and his eyes would look like he had been on a six week drinking binge. But he was a sure enough tough good horse.

Roddy stayed along the creek to cut the cattle off from crossing on one of the few trails that crossed Calamity, and the rest of us made a sweep down that open side. Sure enough, we jumped 17 cows and a few yearlings that were in the pasture. Sam was on the left point, Don was on the left side, and I was on drag. We headed them toward the Highway 118 fence and were going to turn them to the right and take them down the fence. I should have swapped places with Sam, but everything seemed to be going pretty good with the cows hitting a fair trot heading straight for the fence. About fifty yards before we got to the fence, those good Hereford cows hit a dead run and made a left turn that a parade Marshall would have been proud of. Sam was trying to get there, but that old knot-headed horse of his just bogged his head and went to bucking. A few of the old cows peeled off through us to the left and we let them go. I cut on around Sam and Don and got ahead of the cattle as they went through a little brush patch that was just a little bigger than my hat. I got a count on the cattle that went into the brush and there were 13 of them. I got them stopped and turned around and drove them through the brush. As I was riding through, I saw a horse's head over the top of the brush. I figured it was one of Roddy's old mares that I had seen in the pasture earlier. When I got clear of the brush I saw that the horse had a bridle and saddle on him and recognized Sam's knot-headed horse. I hollered at Sam to see if he was alright and he said he was. I saw Don go after the knot-headed horse so I stayed with the cattle. I got another count on the cows and I realized I was missing one. When Don and Sam caught up, I asked Sam to go back and see if he could roust the other cow out of the brush. Don and I started up the fence with the other 12 head and Roddy came to meet us. We got the cattle through the fence, and Sam caught back up to us. He said that the knot-headed horse couldn't keep a fence post from running plumb out of the country. Somebody asked him what happened to him in that brush earlier and he said that the knot-head had turned upside down in a hole that he could fit into, but the knot-head couldn't, so Sam was under the horse upside down in the hole. He said he wiggled his way out, got the horse turned back over and after looking himself and his horse over, he found that neither one of them was hurt.

Roddy figured that if we worked the open side of the creek again, we might get lucky and jump one or two more of the old cows and get a rope on them. We spread out again and started south checking the little patches of brush that we came to. We got pretty close to where we had lost the other cows when I saw Roddy take off at a dead run, swinging his rope over his head. I took off after him and saw that he was in after a cow with another cow and a yearling splitting off to the left. Just as Roddy looked like he was going to throw, he took off to the left and the cow took off to the right. I didn't know what was going on, so I took in after Roddy to see what he was up to. When I got fairly close to where I had last seen him, he came walking out from behind the bush afoot. I hollered at him to see if he was all right and he said he was. I asked him where his horse was and he said he didn't know and didn't care. I asked him which direction the horse went and he said south, so I took off tracking his horse. It wasn't hard tracking the horse because you could see rope marks in the dirt on the right side of the horse tracks. Pretty quick, the tracks hit a dirt road and as I was following the tracks I heard somebody holler. I looked out in the brush, and there stood Sam Dove sitting on that knot-headed horse tied to a mad cow.

I never did figure out how Sam got close enough to a cow on that knot-head to get a rope on her, but he had and was sure wanting some help. I figured Roddy would be all right for the time being and Sam needed me more than Roddy needed his horse. I got a heel loop on one foot of that cow three times, but never could catch both feet because of the heavy brush. Sam got disgusted and said to let him try to tail the cow down. When Sam got hold of the cow's tail, I spurred Bigun and he pulled that cow real good. Bigun also pulled Sam's saddle right up behind Knot-head's ears with the girth jerking his head and forefeet nearly together. That was too much for that green horse, so he started to try to buck. Course he couldn't cause he was all tied up so he just stopped. Sam eased up to him untied my rope from around his saddle horn, and turned that wild cow loose. The hondo (the loop that the rope goes through) was about half way up the side of the cow's neck and the brush kept flipping the rope up even higher. I was able to run up beside the cow and get hold of the rope. Sam had gotten his saddle back where it belonged, caught up to me, and helped me herd the old cow out to a little opening. About the time that we got the cow clear of the brush, we saw Don riding up with Roddy walking beside him. As they approached, a yearling jumped out of the brush between us. I hollered at Sam that I had the cow if he thought he might catch the yearling. Sam and Don hit the brush in hot pursuit.

Roddy came walking up to me and told me to go ahead and get the cow down. I let the cow get her front feet over the rope, then I went the other way. Her legs folded and Roddy jumped on her and tied her feet and said we'd come back with the trailer and load her later. After some debate about either going to get the truck or going to get Roddy's horse, we decided that he would ride double with me. Now I didn't really think too much of that idea and figured that Bigun would think even less of that idea because he had never carried double as far as I knew. He sometimes had a tendency to look and feel like he had a watermelon under the saddle when things weren't going like he expected them to. Roddy told me not to worry because that horse couldn't throw us both off. He may have been right because Roddy weighted about 240 and I weighed about 170. We got the old horse next to an old tank dump; I got a good hold on my reins; Roddy stepped on board. Bigun had a watermelon under the saddle alright, but I kept his head up as we tippy toed around the bottom of that old dry tank. Roddy said that he was alright and for me to quit fooling around and go find his horse. I asked him what had happened that he would find himself afoot. Roddy said everything was going fine up to the point he got ready to throw his rope. He pulled on that yellow horse to check him just a bit, and when he did, he pulled the mechanical hackamore right up and over the horse's ears when the chin strap broke. The old pony just grabbed another gear, quit tracking the cow, and speeded up. Roddy set the bridle on the saddle horn, slipped a loop around the horse's neck, and was fixing to build a rope halter when he looked up and saw the forty foot drop off of Calamity Creek quickly approaching. He just stepped off and slid for home base with the hopes that he didn't go over the bank with his horse. Of course neither he nor the horse did that. That old pony jabbed both front feet into the bank of that creek about eight inches deep and stopped. Then he whirled around and left at a dead run. We went back and looked at the tracks later on and if Roddy hadn't stepped off the horse when he did, there's no doubt both of them would have gone right off the edge. It looked like someone had dragged a truck tire right up to the edge.

I finally decided that Bigun might be ready to carry both of us out of that brush pile, so I started him through the brush. My leggin's would scratch the brush and Bigun would be fine, but as soon as Roddy's leggin's would scratch the brush, Bigun would try to pitch. I'd pull on Bigun's head to get it up and Roddy would pull on the saddle horn to keep us on the saddle. Now like I said Roddy weighed about 240 pounds and every time he squeezed that saddle horn, he squeezed me along with it and would nearly break my ribs. I was so sore the next day that I could hardly breathe.

We finally caught up to Roddy's horse and Roddy said he figured that we had all about used up our luck for the day and also figured that we had better quit before some of us had a run of real bad luck and got ourselves or our horses killed graveyard dead.

There's Good Horses and Bad Horses

I don't remember at what age I rode my first horse, but I do remember the first one that throwed me. I was about 4 years old at the time. My Daddy kept a little black half Shetland mare named Shelt around for us kids to ride. She was pretty gentle most of the time until Daddy decided to breed her. She got kind of obnoxious for a while, but it may have been because there were six of us kids riding her all the time. One day I was riding double behind my brother Lynn on Shelt. She bogged her head and threw me off into a pile of cleared mesquite tree trunks and limbs. I had on the first pair of new boots that I ever owned. They were bright read with a star on the top. My folks had bought them a little big so that I would be able to wear them a little longer. One of those boots set sail when that mare decided to unload. Landing in the brush skinned my face up on one side and it took a long while for it to heal up. We searched the whole area for that boot for about two weeks and never found it. I missed those boots. It upset me a lot more to lose those boots than it did when I skinned up my face. Hide heals; boots cost money.

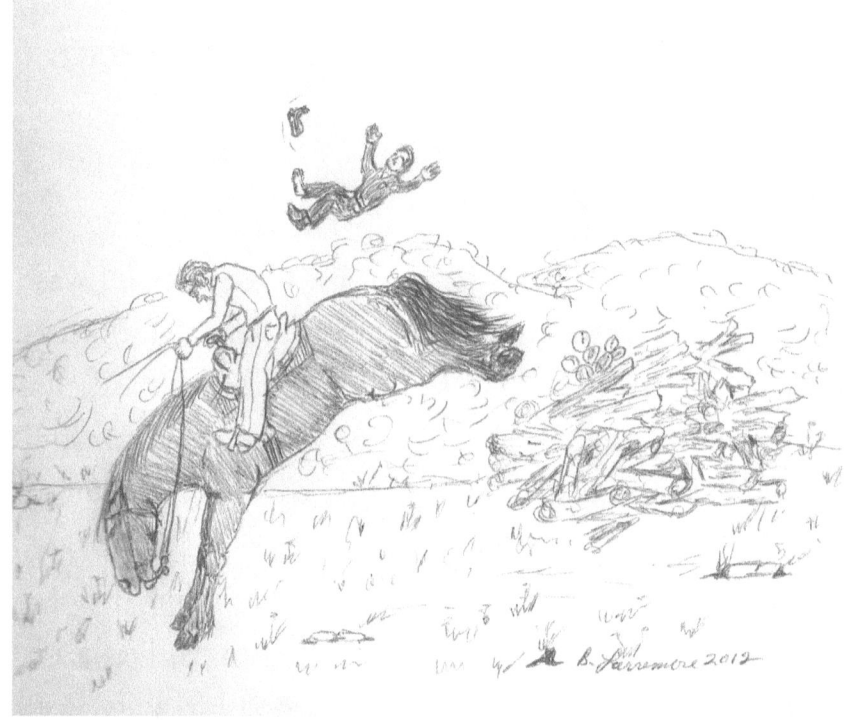

Lynn and me on Shelt. There goes my boot!!

I took another spill on Shelt about a year later and I grew terrified to be around a horse. It took me about 5 years and several horses later before I got comfortable around horses again. Since then, I've known some good horses and some bad horses, some knuckle-heads, and some horses that were naturally gentle as lambs.

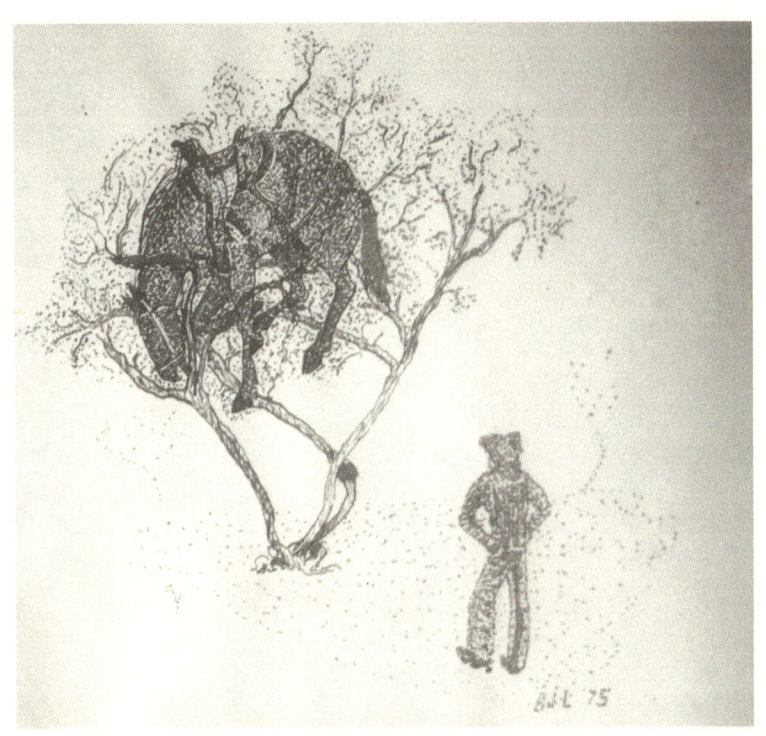

Camel up a tree

CAMEL

Now most folks look at me like they want to call me a liar when I tell this one, but it's the gospel truth. When I was working a ranch in south Texas I had a colt I called Camel. He earned that name cause he traveled like a camel, kind of lumbering from side to side in a trot, a lope, or a walk and was nearly as big. He stood about 15.2 hands and weighted about 1150 pounds and he was only two years old. I'd ridden him about 4 or 5 saddles and had him going pretty good without him bucking. This one day I saddled him up, turned him around the pens a few times then started outside the pens with him. I'd ridden about three or four hundred yards when he went to bucking down the road. It took about three jumps for him to get wound up good with me trying to pull him up. When he got to getting pretty high, he headed for the brush. Now in south Texas, the mesquite brush ranges somewhere from knee high to thirty feet up. Well, Camel decided he could clear a tree about twenty feet high and tried it before I could do anything about it. He didn't quite make it. He came straight down in the middle of that spread out tree. He caught enough limbs coming down that he stopped about eight feet off the ground with me still sitting in the saddle. I sure did feel silly way up there in the air horseback with nothing between me and the ground but a tree. He started wiggling but couldn't get anything done, so I climbed down on another limb and looked the situation over. The only way that I could see to get him out of that tree was the same way he went in. I climbed back up to him and threw my long rope reins out of the tree over his rump. I climbed back out of the tree, grabbed the reins and pulled and ran. The first thing that hit the ground was the saddle horn, and then Camel hit the ground on the back of his head. I grabbed him as he came up and kept him from running off. He looked around kind of wild-eyed and finally settled down, but he was alright. He never offered to buck again. I guess he figured that bucking and the treetops were for the birds and not for ignorant young horses.

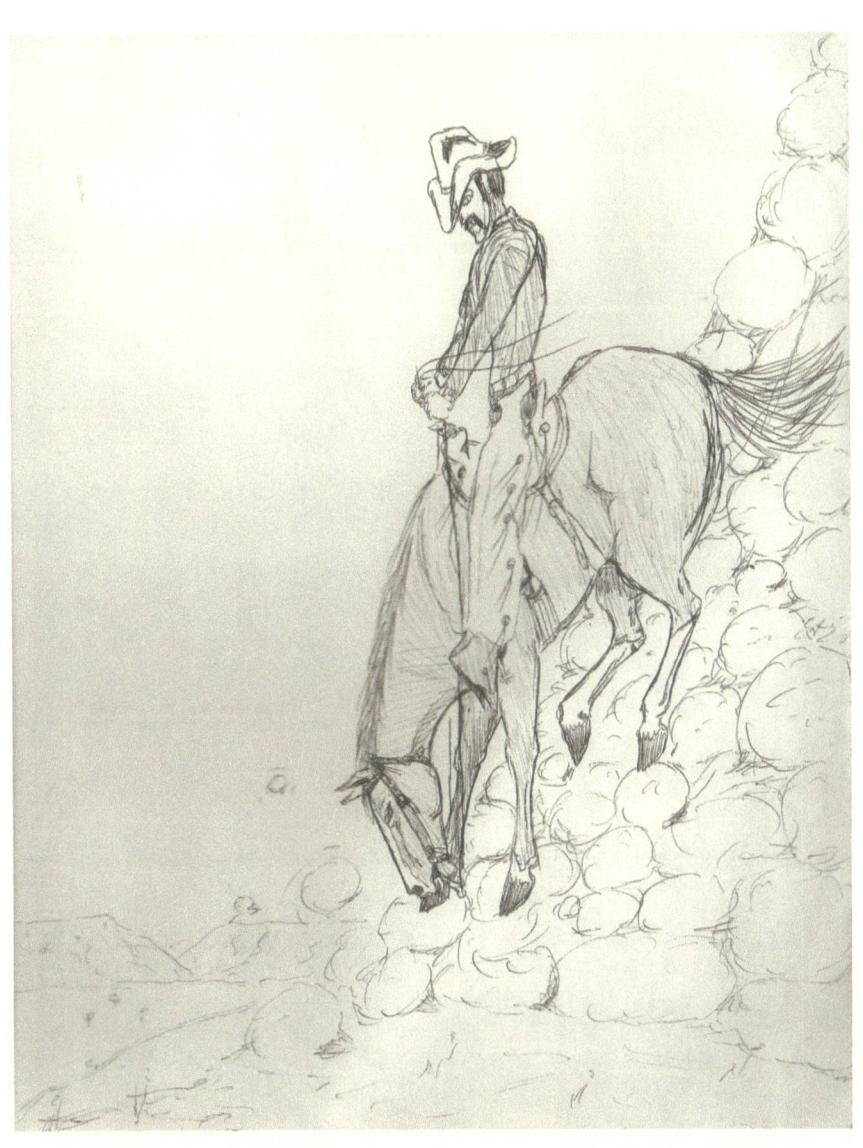

Toddy coming down the Elephant Mountain benches

TODDY

My Daddy found a colt on the Falls Creek Ranch in Llano County back in 1969 that he thought I might want. I had broken some of their colts before and liked the horses that they raised. This colt was out of a thoroughbred mare and a quarter-horse stud. He didn't have any papers, but I've never seen anybody saddle a set of papers, ride off on them, or do a day's work on them, so that didn't bother me. He was raised in the rocks and brush, which he needed where he was going. I asked my Dad to get him for me and the next time Dad came to Alpine, he brought him. He was a sorrel, blaze faced colt with two back stockings and eventually grew to be 15.2 hands and weighed about 1250 pounds. He moved a whole lot like a panther, with a smooth quick feline motion. I called him Tennessee Toddy. Toddy for short.

I broke him when he was a two-year old. He got madder than an old wet hen when I staked him out and he turned on me and charged with hoofs slashing and baby teeth popping. I got out of his way and let him settle down some and after he did, he broke out real nice. In two weeks, he was handling pretty good and I was carrying baby calves, milk buckets, hoes, shovels, or anything else that I wanted to on him. Leanna, my daughter, was two at the time, and when I would come in from the pasture on him, I would stop at the house and set her up on Toddy and lead him up to the barn. I did this several times and the colt never paid any attention to Leanna on his back. One day I got the pair of them about half way up to the barn when Leanna reached down and kicked the stirrup leathers of my saddle. The colt nearly jumped in the middle of me, squatted, and stood there trembling. I eased back and pulled the baby off from where she was hanging on to the saddle horn. I should have let him smell her and put her back on, but the whole thing boogered me. From that day on, Toddy was terrified of kids. They just flat scared him to death.

I left him a stud until he was a four-year old. He'd stay with a cow all day long and work all day, every day as long as you wanted to put your saddle on him. I would have put him up against anybody's horse when it came to cutting a herd. I never bred him to anything but an old white jenny that I kept to pack deer on. He got the idea that anything with long ears ought to be romantically inclined to accept him.

I took him down to Dub Yarbourgh's place where my brother, Gary, was working to help gather their cattle. The foreman had a college boy, Ted Yadon, working that day that had partied a little long into the night and who had as big a hangover as I ever saw. The foreman put this little feller on a nice little smooth walking mule so maybe he could get some work out of him. When that mule stepped out from behind the barn, Toddy perked up and paid attention. I gave him a little slack and headed their way. That little hungover cowboy went to whipping and spurring that little mule. I would give Toddy just enough slack to keep him from catching that mule and after we ran them a ways and really had their attention, I pulled Toddy up. Toddy wasn't happy about it and never did figure out that the mule wouldn't have done him any good, because it was a gelding.

During that time, I had stomach ulcers and pretty bad ones. I kept eggnog with me all the time cause it would sooth my ulcers some. I would take a swig out of that bottle of eggnog and that hungover kid kept watching me and kept getting more and more thirsty. He finally asked me what it was and I told him that it was a sure fire cure for hangovers. He said that he'd sure admire to have a drink of it. We aggravated one another about it for awhile and I finally told him it was raw eggs and milk. Ted stepped off his mule and commenced to throwing up. I never have seen anyone throw up as much as that kid did and I couldn't help but laugh.

I had a Blue Lacy dog named Bo that put in a number of miles with Toddy and me. Whenever Toddy would go out of the pens, Bo would run up behind him and nip him on the heels. One day Toddy got enough of it, whirled, and before Bo could get away, Toddy pawed him. He caught just the very tip of Bo's tail at an angle and Toddy's horseshoe sliced off the end of the tail. Bo may have nipped at other horses after that, but he never bothered Toddy again.

Roddy Schoenfeld, the Ranch foreman of the Elephant Mountain Ranch, called me one spring and asked if I could help him gather a bunch of cross-bred Brahma heifer yearlings and take them up an old road to the top. Like a fool, I said I would. Elephant Mountain is just what it's name sounds like. Big and grey. It climbs up out of Chalk Valley on the east side nearly straight up for about 6800 feet. This old road was nearly all switch-backs from bench to bench as it stair-stepped to the top. Between each set of benches was a pile of boulders from the size of my head to the size of a house.

These heifers were a little ringy or what you would call unsociable. They weren't really wild, but they made us do a good bit of riding before we got them together to start them to the top of the mountain. By the time we got half way up the mountain, Toddy was about the only one with any juice left. Most of the other cowboys with us were leading their horses and driving the cattle afoot. When the heifers got about two-thirds of the way up, about 50 head decided that they liked it better at the bottom a whole lot better. They proceeded to the bottom without taking the road. The cows would just drop off of one bench onto another, run across it, and keep going. When they got down to Toddy and me, Toddy did his best to stop them, but they were on a roll and just flowed around us like we were stones in a flood of water. Toddy whirled and sailed out after them, jumping sliding, then catching himself just enough to jump again. He'd reach the next bench about 40 to 60 feet down by hitting it once, then bounding down to the next. I'd just pucker up; pray real fast, and tell that old pony that if he didn't stay on his feet, we'd both wind up in a hot place with a pair of broken necks. About five or six benches down, I finally decided that even Toddy wasn't going to be able to stop the first few head of cows because they were still flying from one bench to the other like a bunch of crows landing in a corn field. Finally, Toddy got some of the slower cows held up and back to the road and we started back up. Toddy and me took about 40 head back up the mountain all by ourselves. I was sure proud of that horse.

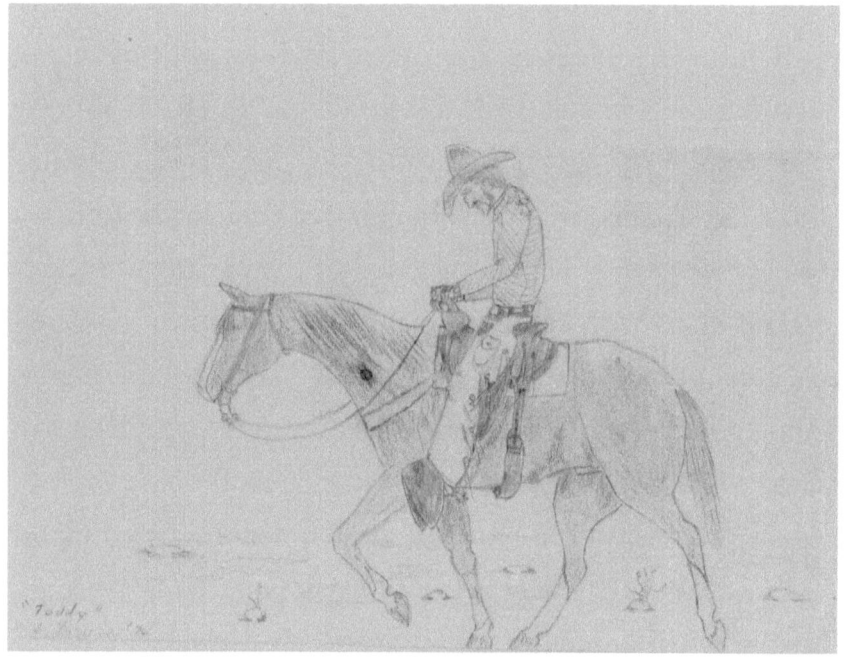

Toddy, the best horse I ever had

I was still suffering from ulcers during that time and I still carried some eggnog with me, but without the nog, in a stainless steel thermos. It was actually a Dr. Pepper float. This particular day, the owner's wife was riding with us and she kept watching me every time I took a swig out of that thermos. She had no idea what I was drinking.

After a while she rode up to Roddy and told him that a man was drinking on the job. Roddy didn't have the heart to tell her that her wild west Texas cowboy was drinking a Dr. Pepper shake instead of whiskey, so he just told her that help was hard to find and until I had too much, I was a pretty fair hand, and he kept hiring me in spite of my bad habits. I guess the poor lady still thinks that I'm a sot drunk. By the way, I haven't had a drop of alcohol in more than 30 years!

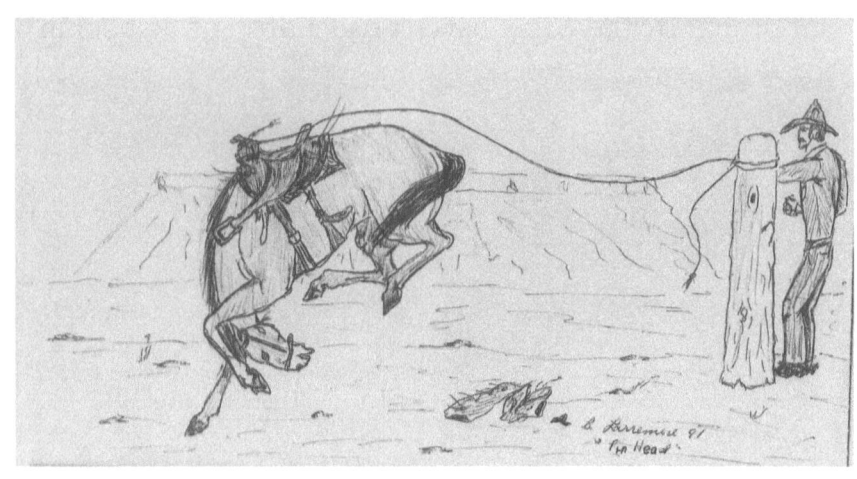

Pinhead, one ugly horse

PINHEAD

One spring, we had all our horses eating Loco weed.
I put all the horses in the pen and fed them until I could
get the weed dug out of our horse traps. One of the traps
was easy to get to with a trailer and we were loading all
the Loco that we dug there and hauling it to Sul Ross
State University in Alpine, so they could run experiments
with it on some cattle. The other trap lay in an old deep
canyon, so we just dug the Loco and let it rot. Once a
horse gets Loco, they are never the same and can get
real mean and crazy; they don't even know what they are
doing. I kept several younger horses in the canyon after
I thought that the Loco had dried up enough to where
the horses wouldn't eat it. That was one of the worst
mistakes I ever made in my life. The dried Loco seemed
to affect the horses quicker than the green stuff, and
the horses seemed to like it even better. I saved all the
younger horses, but within a week after putting the other

horses in the canyon, they all became affected. I had to sell the best horses that I had ever had.

I started looking for other horses and all I could find was 3 unbroke colts. One of them I didn't really want, but went ahead and took because 3 of them were cheaper than two. The third colt was pretty good and was good looking if you cut his head off right behind his ears. His ears came out of his head about an inch apart and nearly crossed at the tops. His forehead bulged out under that and his eyes bulged out of their sockets with the whites showing all the way around them. His nose would have put the Roman war gods to shame. His lower lip drooped about two inches below the top lip and he had a very little jawbone. I may have seen uglier headed horses in my time, but I sure don't remember them. I named him Pinhead.

My belly was acting up right smart, so I didn't figure that I could stand to break and train three colts at a time, so I got Sam Dove to ride the colts for a couple of weeks for me one at a time. I figured that Pinhead would give the most trouble, so I sent him first. I told Sam that I didn't care if he taught them much, just as long as he kind of got the buck out of them. In a little over two weeks, Sam called me and told me that Pinhead was ready. Pinhead would turn on a dime, stand for you to get on and off either side, and come to a real nice sliding stop. Sam had done a superb job of putting a handle on him. Sam said the little horse would run cows better than he handled, but there might be one little problem. He just never could seem to get the little horse to where he didn't like to pitch. I told him that I'd go ahead and take him home and see what I could get done. I rode him every day for the next six weeks. I'd warm him up under the saddle every morning before I got on him and when I did get on him, I'd point him straight up a mountain and go to the top with him. I didn't have any trouble with him for about six weeks. That little horse would watch and work a cow like an old ranch horse. He had a nice little running walk and a fox trot that would just make you giggle. He was starting to turn into a cowboy's dream if you could just forget about that fool head on him.

One morning I saddled him up, warmed him up a little, and went to the top of the mountain. After I topped out, we were easing through some rocks, brush, and cactus when I guess I got a little impatient. I just barely touched him with a spur and he exploded. He'd leave the ground facing one direction, do a 360 degree turn in the air and land facing the same direction he'd started in. I kept telling him that he wasn't going to throw me off in that pile of rocks and cactus. I actually began to believe it myself! Every time that he hit the ground, he would change directions. I started anticipating him and about the twelfth or fourteenth jump, he didn't change directions. He stuck my head in that rock and cactus pile just like I'd been telling him that he wasn't going to do. He bucked about a hundred yards into the middle of a little bunch of cows, threw up his head, gathered up the cows, and drove them to a water trough about a half mile away. Damndest thing I ever saw. When I caught up to Pinhead, he was still holding the cattle up at the water trough. I never got on him again that he didn't at least crow-hop with me. More often, he would buck like a scalded dog. If I could keep him circling in one direction, I could ride him. If I ever turned his head loose, he'd generally pile drive me again and disappear out from under me. This kept up until an old mare kicked my front teeth out and I had to have the rest of my top teeth pulled. After that, whenever Pinhead would buck with me, he'd drive my bottom teeth up into those top gums and nearly take the top of my head off. I began to worry about having to get on him the next morning and it finally got so bad that I'd lay awake nights dreading having to ride him. You might say he was starting to get into bed with me. I tried to sell that colt a few times, but nobody would buy him, not even the rodeo outfits. I finally decided that since I was going to have to keep him, I'd just have to ride him myself. I figured, I'd better start teaching him not to buck.

On a Friday morning, I saddled him up and tied a good nylon rope from a good stout cedar post to his hobbles. Just as I got ready to throw a pair of leggings under him, Luther came out of the house with a suggestion. He said that an old man on the Brown Ranch would break a mean bucking horse by tying a rope to the saddle horn and to the top of a good stout cedar post and just let him buck. Luther said that I'd have to watch the rope to keep the horse from getting tangled up in it. I thought I could manage that and rerigged my rope the way Luther told me to and took Pinhead's hobbles off. I threw my leggings up under the horse and he didn't need much more incentive than that. He bogged his head and headed for the moon. When he hit the end of the rope, his feet flew right straight out and wound up parallel to his body. He didn't hit the ground. I never have figured out how he did it but he landed on his feet. He had to do it against a stretched nylon rope tied to the saddle horn, but he did it. It just made him mad. Every time that he would hit the end of the rope, he would buck a little harder and bawl a little louder. He hit the end of it about a dozen times but never went down. The last time he hit the end of the rope he did finally go down and hit the ground. It wasn't because he got tangled up in the rope, but when he got up, I saw he'd broken his leg up in the stifle. I had to put him down and I've always regretted having to do that. He would have made a great horse if I could have stayed with him.

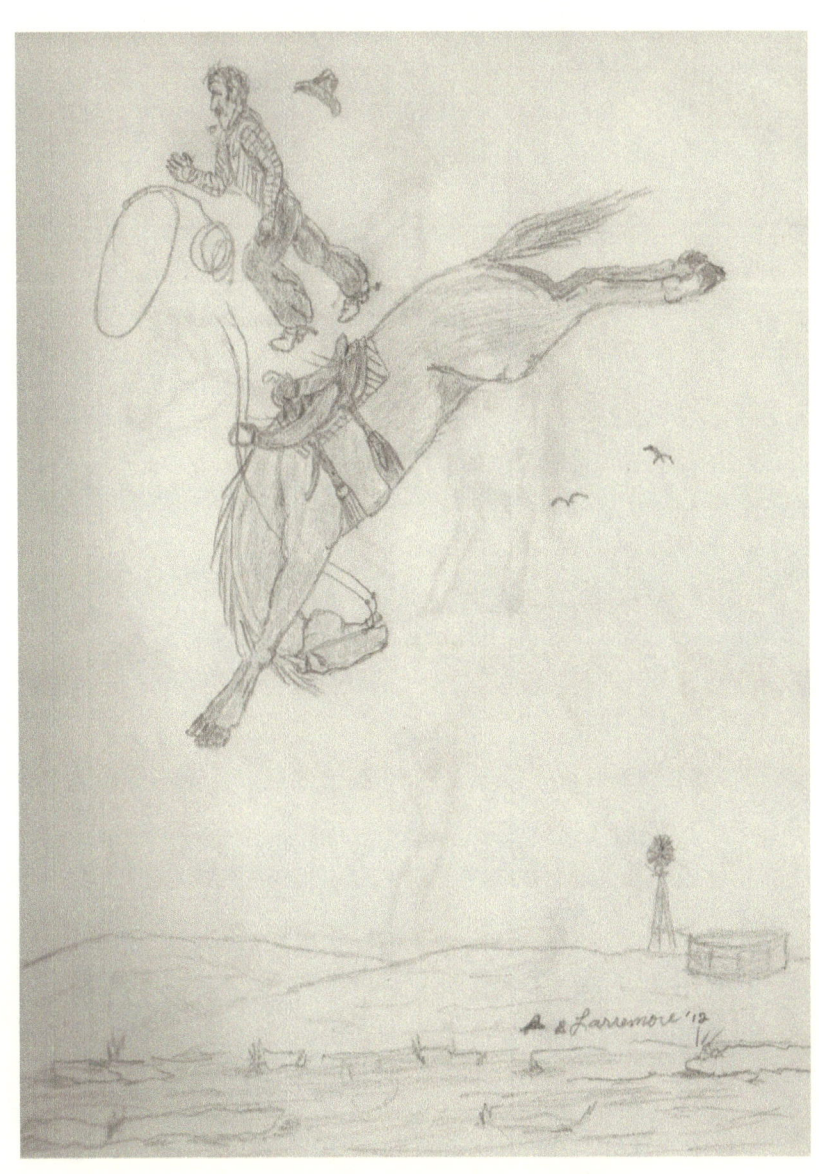

Pump Jack and me flying high

PUMP JACK

Like I said, there are some good horses and there are some bad horses, then there's just horses. Pump Jack was a hell of a horse, but we did have our wrecks. I got Pump Jack by trading Bigun when he was 9 years old to Apache Adams. Pump Jack was a 3 year old when I traded for him and was fresh broke with about 20 saddles and fresh castrated. He was all legs, head, and feet. Like I said earlier, he looked like every time he took a step he was going to lift his rear off the ground. By the time he was 5, he grew into those legs, feet, and head and grew to about 16.2 hands high and weighed about 1350 pounds. I moved to Corona, New Mexico, as foreman on Bogles Mashed O sheep, cattle, and goat ranch. We were gathering buck sheep and had one old ewe that wouldn't cut out of the bunch of bucks. I told my men we would just take the old ewe through the gate, rope her and drag her back. I took in after the ewe and Pump Jack wasn't wanting to track her. I got to eating on him pretty heavy with my spurs and he blew up with me. Prior to that every time he tried to buck, he'd get those long legs tangled up and just quit bucking in disgust. Well, he had grown up. He went as high as any horse ever bucked with me. When he got to the top of that first jump, he took a high dive and just flicked me like a booger just that much higher. I must have been 40 feet up in the air. It took a long time to come down. I landed on both knee caps on a big flat rock. Dan Chavez caught Pump Jack for me and another man roped the sheep and drug it through the gate. Pump Jack was so tall they had to help me get back on him because both knee caps were busted. Dan Chavez was a short-legged man, but I as tall as I was and when he started colts the first thing he'd teach them was to stretch out so he could get on. He said it was easier to get on and besides it took the horse longer to stand up before he could buck. Dan taught me how to make one stretch out and as long as I kept Pump Jack, I'd make him stretch out so I could get on him easier.

When I sold him because of old age, I led him into the sale ring, made him stretch out, stepped on him and I heard people in the crowd say, "did you see how he got on that horse?" That and the looks of the old horse brought $1500.00 which was top of the market for horses at that time.

One day I was working up at Sul Ross University and trying to run the Larremore-Anderson Ranch and had a bunch of deer hunters come down. When I'd come in from work, I'd go out and visit with them to see how the hunting had gone. Every day they would tell me they had seen a lion, shot at him, and missed. I told them to quit shooting at em' and start shooting them after about the third day. The forth day, an elderly gentleman told me he had shot a lion, thought he had hit it, but that it had gone in some brush and as he was by himself, he was leery of going into the brush pile after it. He told me where it was in a deep old canyon, under a bluff, over a rockslide. I told the hunters I'd take my dogs and go to the canyon and meet them there the next morning. I left the hunters headed toward the canyon, took a short cut and got to the bluff. I waited for them about 30 minutes, but they never showed up. I found their tracks later where they had gotten about half way there, turned around and left. I never saw them again. Apparently they pulled out and left the ranch. I tied my horse to a pretty stout bush, took off my leggings and coat and crawled down around the edge of the bluff to the top of the rock slide.

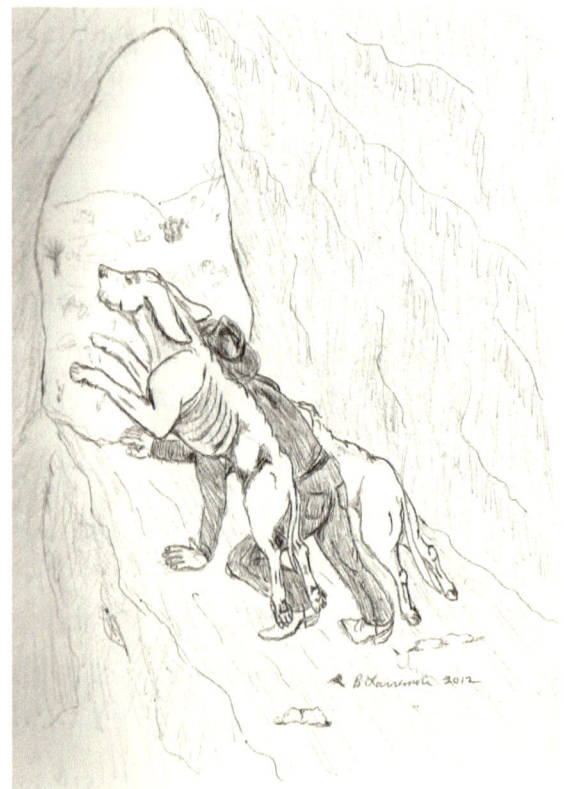

Carl Potter and his dogs coming out of a cave

My dogs went ahead of me along the top of the rock slide with me following. They went into a bunch of brush and I guess that lion was in there asleep and one of the dogs bit him on the rear. That lion jumped straight up in the air and screamed like a banshee. My feet went pitty-pat the other direction. I did not tell my feet to go pitty-pat the other direction, but they did. I took four or five running steps and thought to myself, "you fool, you got a gun, you better turn around and see what's about to catch you!" The lion was running down the rock slide with my dogs after him. They crossed a short flat and I took a shot at the lion but he swerved and I hit right where he should have been. He went into some trees along the draw at the bottom of the canyon. I could see he didn't come out the other side of the canyon, but couldn't tell if he went up or down or stopped. I eased down to where my dogs were circling through the trees, but they didn't know where he was because they hadn't been trained to tree anything.

Pickles, one of my dogs, kept circling the big cedar tree and I looked it over pretty thoroughly, but there was no lion there. I eased around the cedar tree and there was a big live oak leaning out over the draw. The lion was laying there looking at me. I took careful aim, shot him between the eyes and he was dead when he hit the ground. After that, I've always made sure my dogs know how to tree. I skinned the lion, got back up where I'd tied my horse and the horse was gone. He had buggered from all the shooting and hollering, broke the reins and left the country. I picked up my leggings and coat, tracked the horse back to the last gate we'd gone through and had to ease up to him very carefully, cause I smelled like that lion. I split my reins and tied them back together, wiped my bloody hand across that horse's nose and tied that lion hide behind the saddle. The wind was whipping around and as long as the wind was in front of us, we did alright. When the wind would change to behind us that horse would smell the lion hide, grab himself and want to run or buck. He was light-headed and I kept control of him, and we finally made it back to the house with the lion hide. The ranch was nearly a 10 section ranch and 9 lions were found on that ranch that year and nearly wiped out the deer population.

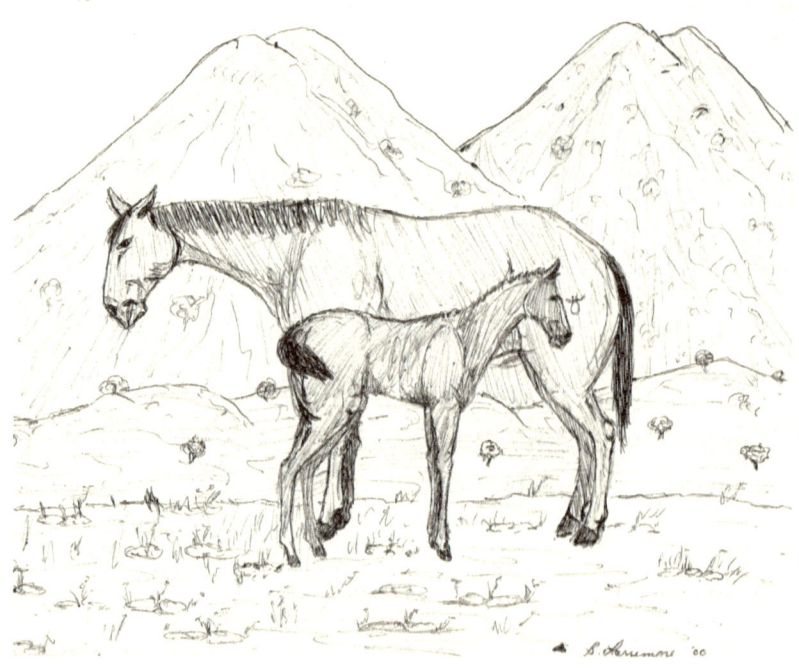

Mare and Colt with Twin Peaks Mountain in back in Alpine, Texas

Jim, Tom T Cat, Bo, and Peaches

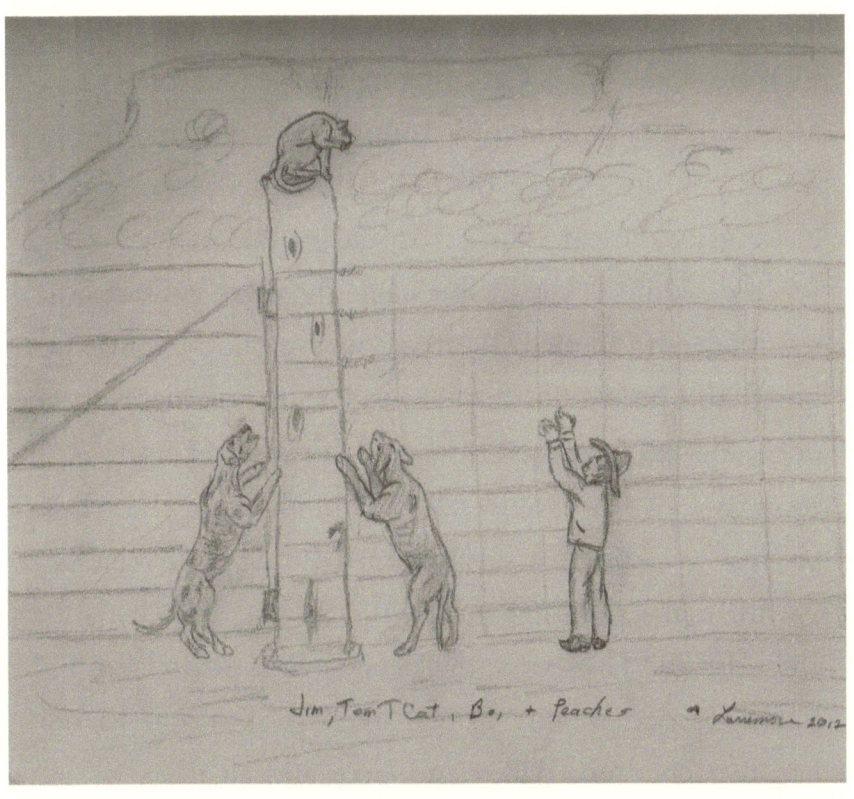

Jim, Tom T Cat, Bo, and Peaches

Jim was born in September 1972. After Leanna, he seemed to be half grown when he was born. He never got treated like a real baby. We lived right around the corner of the canyon where Luther and Tinny lived. Jim would go back and forth through the pens from our house to theirs. We lived outside of Alpine on the Larremore-Anderson Ranch just south of Alpine. When Jim would go for walks, Tom T Cat, Bo, and Peaches would follow. First Peaches, then Bo, and Tom T Cat bringing up the rear. Every now and then, Jim would whirl around and holler and the cat would run up a fence post and Bo and Peaches would chase after the cat. The cat would sit up on top of the fence post and lick his paws while the dogs bounced off the fence and barked. Pretty soon everybody would get bored and Jim would turn around, start walking, call the dogs, and Peaches, then Bo would fall into step and pretty soon Tom T Cat would fall in behind. Then the whole process would repeat several times during their walk.

Jim married Lisa Patrick in 1994 and they had one child, Justin. They were divorced several years later and Jim remarried Mandy Roush in 2001. Jim and Mandy had two children, Bailey and Cole and all three of my grandchildren have been a treasure. Justin stays with his mother in another town.

Jim and Mandy bought a place in Alpine and opened a horse boarding stable with the help of my brother David. Jim took a job as foreman with J. P. Bryant south of Marathon on the Marivillas Ranch to help support the boarding stables. He and Mandy have taught the children how to rope and ride since they were babies. They are surely going to make some great cowboys when they get older.

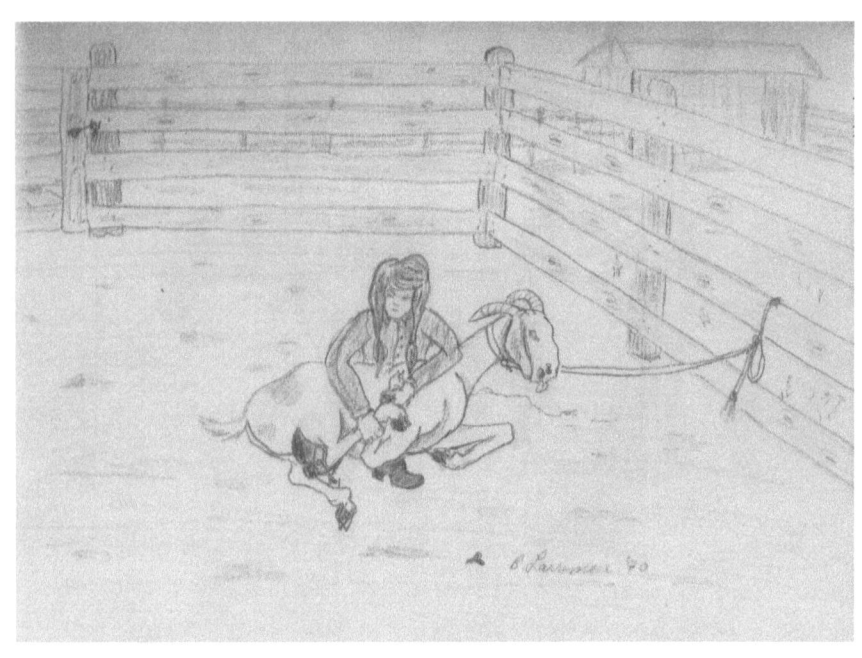

Leanna tying her goat

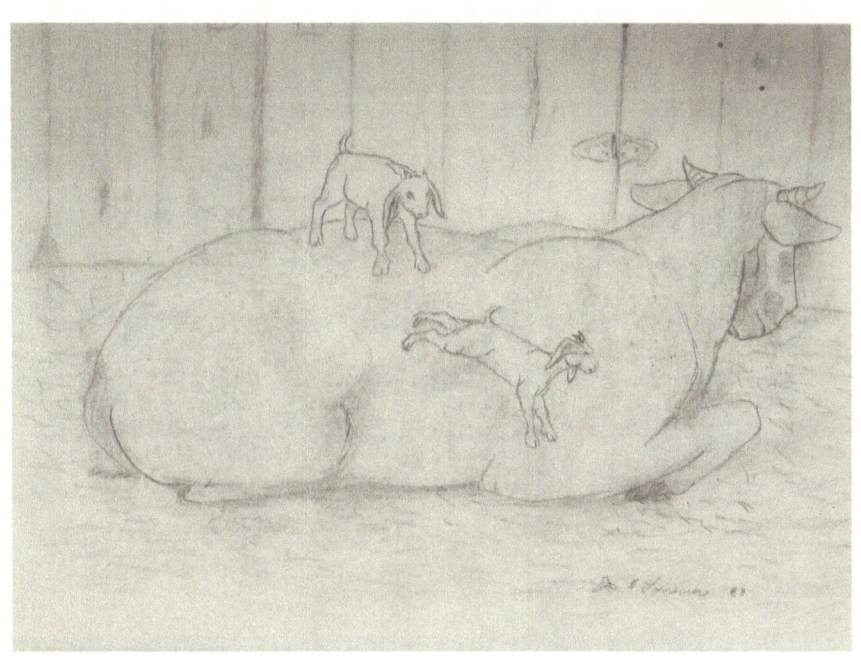

Leanna's baby goats playing "King of the Mountain" on a
steer

Leanna was born in September of 1968. She was born two months premature and had medical problems her whole life. We had to feed every half hour every day for the first four months of her life. I would stay up and take care of her until I couldn't stay up anymore, then Ann would take care of her during the day. We would keep her bassinette near the bed so we could hear her if she woke up. She sounded like a little weak kitten, but she started talking at 7 months and could speak plainly when she was 9 months old. She didn't start walking until she was 2 years old. She was mentally strong, but physically weak, but nothing seemed to stop her from wanting to try something new. As she got older, Leanna never had any fear of anything, would show horses, steers, pigs, goats, or chickens in the FFA and 4H clubs. She always had a book in her hand and read continuously.

When Sugar rolled on me and broke my tail bone, Leanna was about 2 years old. For about 4 days, I couldn't sleep, couldn't stand up, couldn't sit down; I just hurt. The only way I could get comfortable was to put my feet up on her little foot stool that she sat on to watch TV. She came by, saw my feet on her footstool, and jerked it out from under my feet. I felt just like she had castrated me. I screamed, Leanna started crying and Ann came in asking what I'd done to the baby. I said, "nothing, she just damn near killed me!" Ann explained to her that her Daddy needed that footstool so he could sleep. She understood after that and let me use it.

Leanna always had animals around her and started bottle feeding doggie calves when she was 4 or 5. She had this pair of baby goats when we lived in Corona, New Mexico and would watch them play King of the Mountain with this big ol' fat lazy steer I was feeding out. She tried and tried to get pictures of those goats playing on that ol' steer, but every time she would take her camera out to get the picture, the goats would stop playing and run to her. I finally decided to draw the picture for her so she would have the memory of it.

One day, Irvin Caveness was working cows with us. Leanna was about 12 or 13 years old and could ride as good as any cowboy. A bull broke loose from the herd and Irvin went after it and Leanna followed. Irvin said he thought he was going at a pretty good clip until Leanna passed him on Blaze. As Leanna and Blaze passed him, Blaze threw a shoe and it went whizzing by his head right next to his ear. Leanna went ahead and turned the bull by herself and got him back in the herd.

When we moved to Corona, I took a milk cow with us. Her name was Bonnet and she was half Brown Swiss and half Hereford. She was the best milk cow I ever had and was gentle as a dog. She would give 6 gallons of milk a day even after the calf had sucked her out. Apparently when I moved her up into the snow bank in New Mexico, she got mad. When I would milk her, I had a kitten in the barn with me and I would squirt milk in its mouth. I had a three gallon stainless steel milk bucket full of milk one evening, and there was snow on the ground, and it was about 20 degrees. The kitten was standing between Bonnet's back feet. Bonnet moved her foot and stepped on the kitten and the kitten bit Bonnet under the fetlock. Bonnet kicked that bucket with over 3 gallons of milk right square upside down over my head. Jim and Leanna were out tending to their chores and saw it happen. I was wet, cold, and mad. When they burst out laughing, I told them to shut up or I'd whup em'. They broke for the house laughing their heads off. I picked up a two-by-four, hit Bonnie with it, she'd kick and I'd hit her again. In a little bit I could hear Ann laughing outside the pen. I turned around and said "it's not funny." Ann said, "yes it is, from this side of the fence." Then I began to see the humor in the situation.

Leanna passed away when she was 17. She passed away because of medical conditions and I miss her still every day.

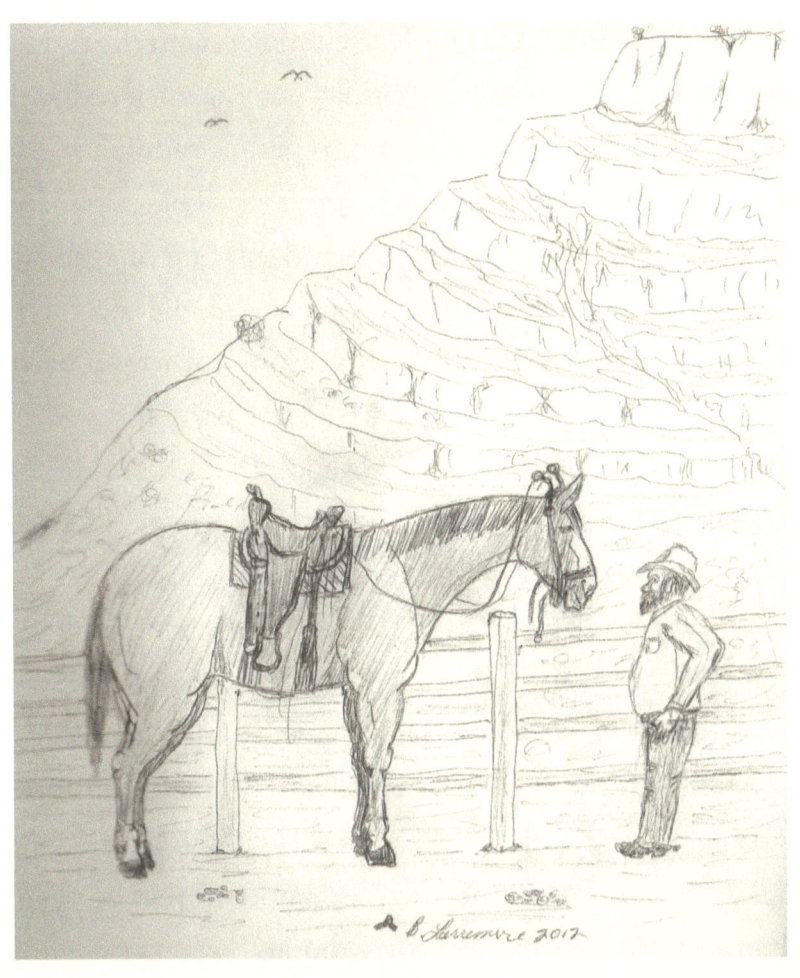

A joke played on Joe

I was neighbor working with Roddy Schoenfeld down at the Elephant Mountain Ranch. Joe Lewis was working for him and Rod Devoll and Sam Dove were day working. Joe went out and found his horse saddled with the saddle put on backwards and his bridle put on upside down. The next morning Joe went out to get his saddle off the rack and it had been nailed to the rack. That night Joe put his saddle under some sacks and put one of Roddy's saddles that looked just like his on the saddle rack. The next morning, Joe, Sam, and Rod went out to the barn, and Joe looked up at the ceiling of the barn and said "I wonder what the boss's saddle is doing up in the rafters of the barn" Rod and Sam had to scramble to get Roddy's saddle out of the rafters before Roddy showed up for work. Joe told Sam and Rod, "boys, I don't get mad, I get even."

When we got through with the works, Joe asked Rod and Sam how they liked the coffee he'd been making every morning. They said they liked it fine, and asked why he was asking. Joe asked them if they'd noticed that he never drank any of it. They said they did and were wondering why he wouldn't drink any of his own coffee. Joe said, "you reckon I've been taking a leak in that coffee every morning?" To this day, I don't think Rod or Sam will drink a cup of coffee if Joe is in the same camp with them.

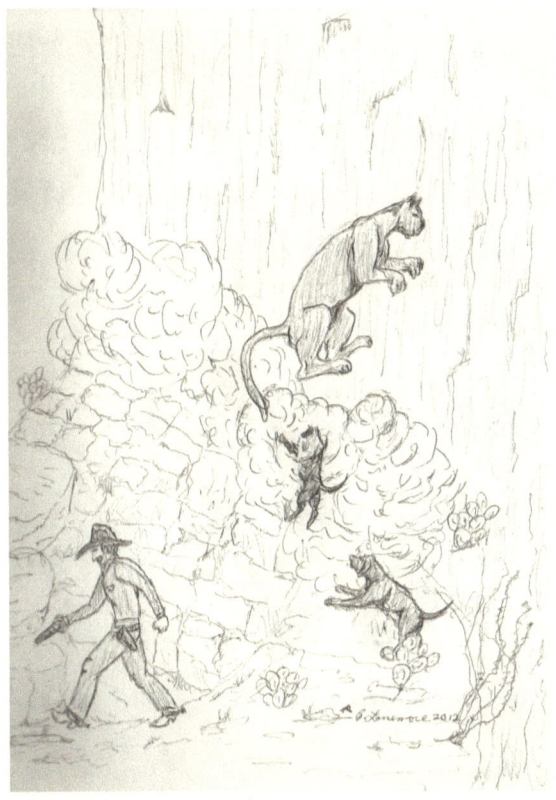

Carl Potter and his dogs coming out of a cave

Carl Potter and his family was trying to run sheep and goats down at Santiago Peak south of Alpine. Lions were coming up out of Big Bend National Park and were killing off his sheep and goats. Carl had a trigg gyp, which is a hound dog. This gyp had a litter pups about half grown and the gyp was a pretty good lion dog. Carl was trying to train the pups to be lion dogs as well. The dogs hit a lion track and followed it down into a cave. Carl followed the dogs into the cave and he heard the lion scream down inside; the pups passed Carl and Carl beat them out of the cave. He gathered the pups and went back into the cave. The lion crawled into another cave and Carl and the dogs followed, but the lion got away.

JUST FOR LAUGHS

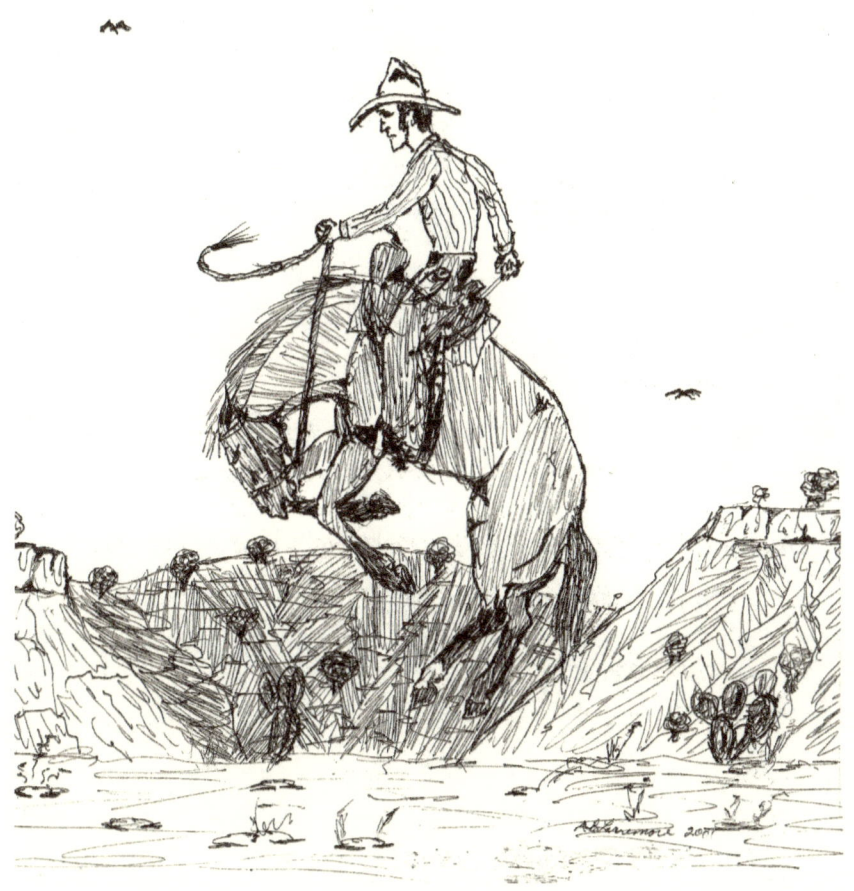

Another wreck

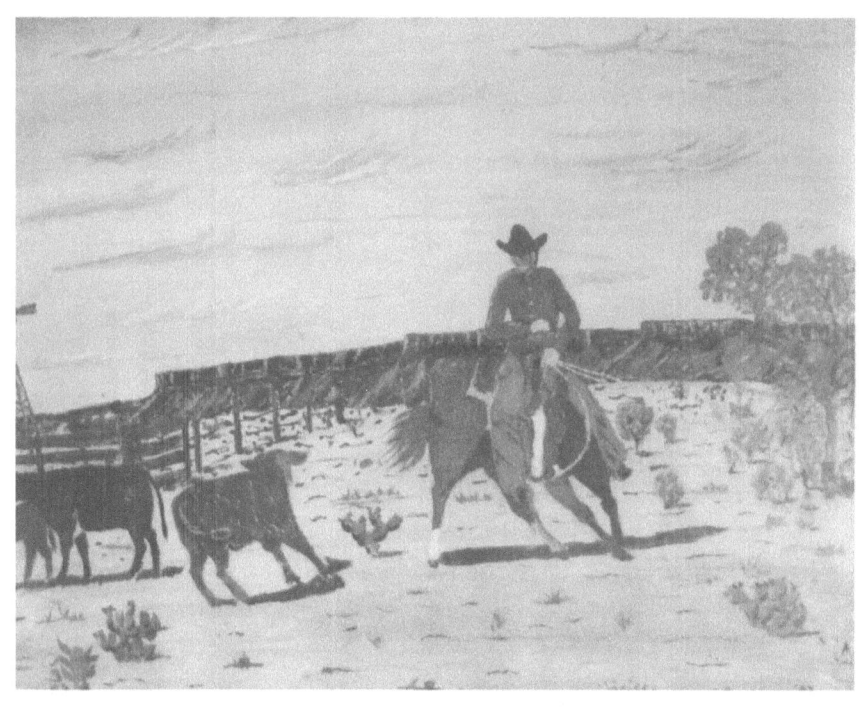

Brian on Dot's at the Larremore Ranch 35 miles south of
Alpine, Texas Kokernot Mesa in the background

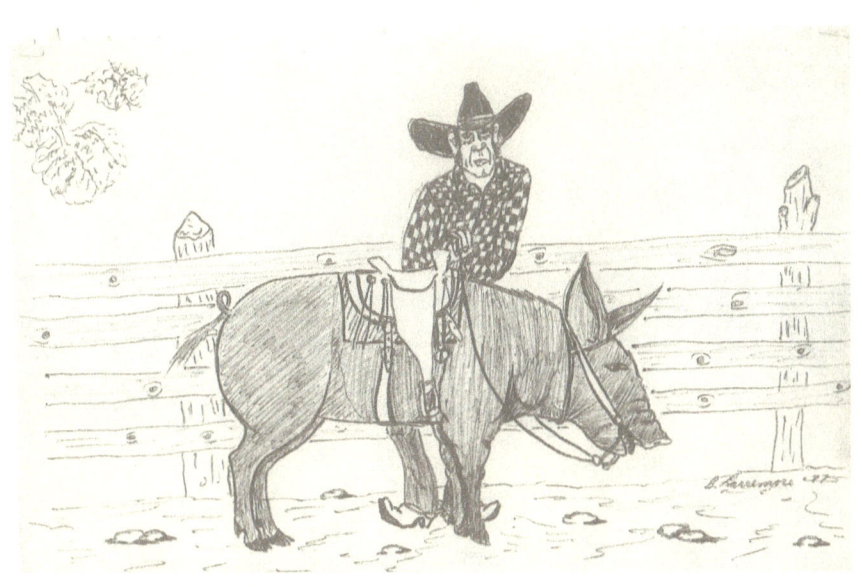

Horse, I think one of us got drunk last night

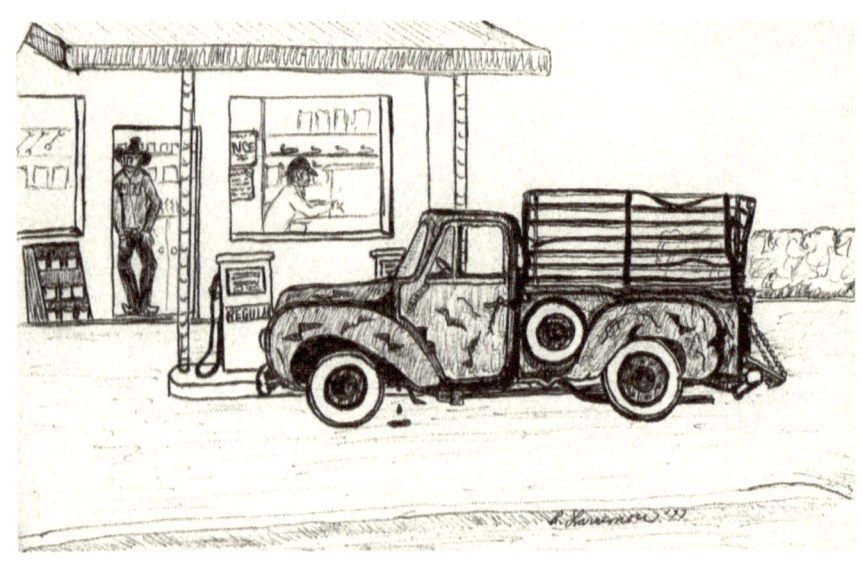

I don't know why Maw thinks we need a new pickup

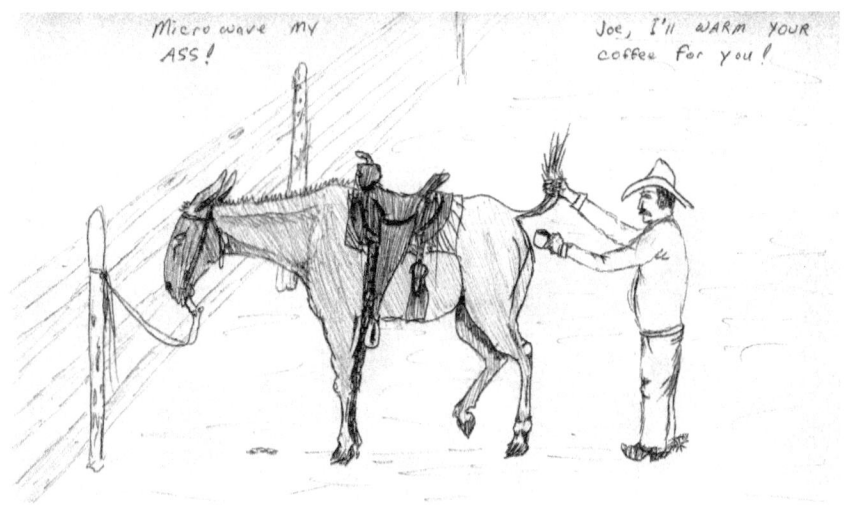

Self explanatory

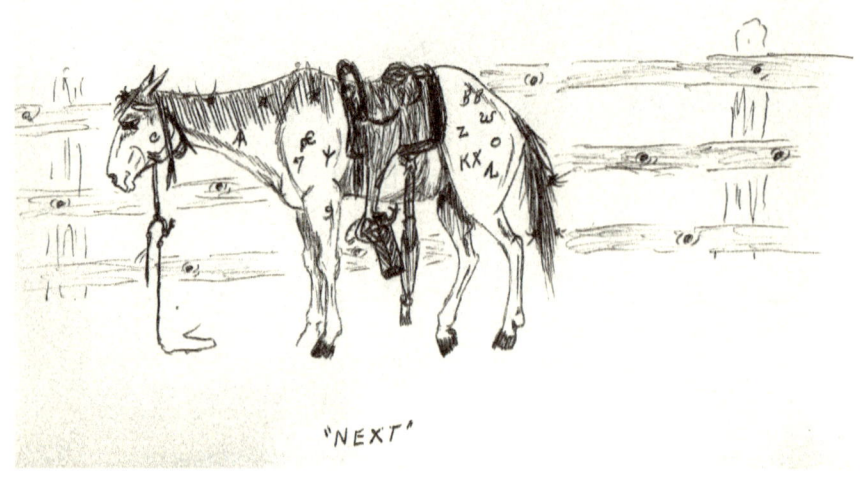

"NEXT"

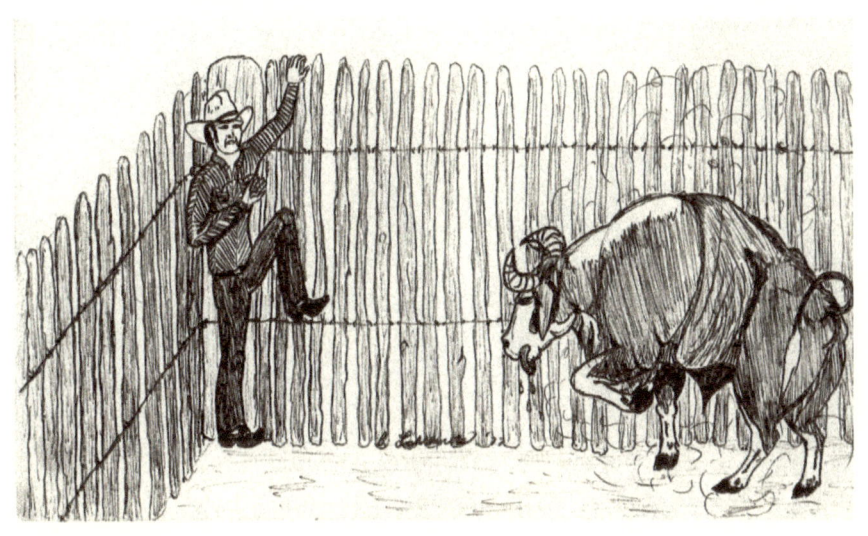

Whoa bull! Nice bull!

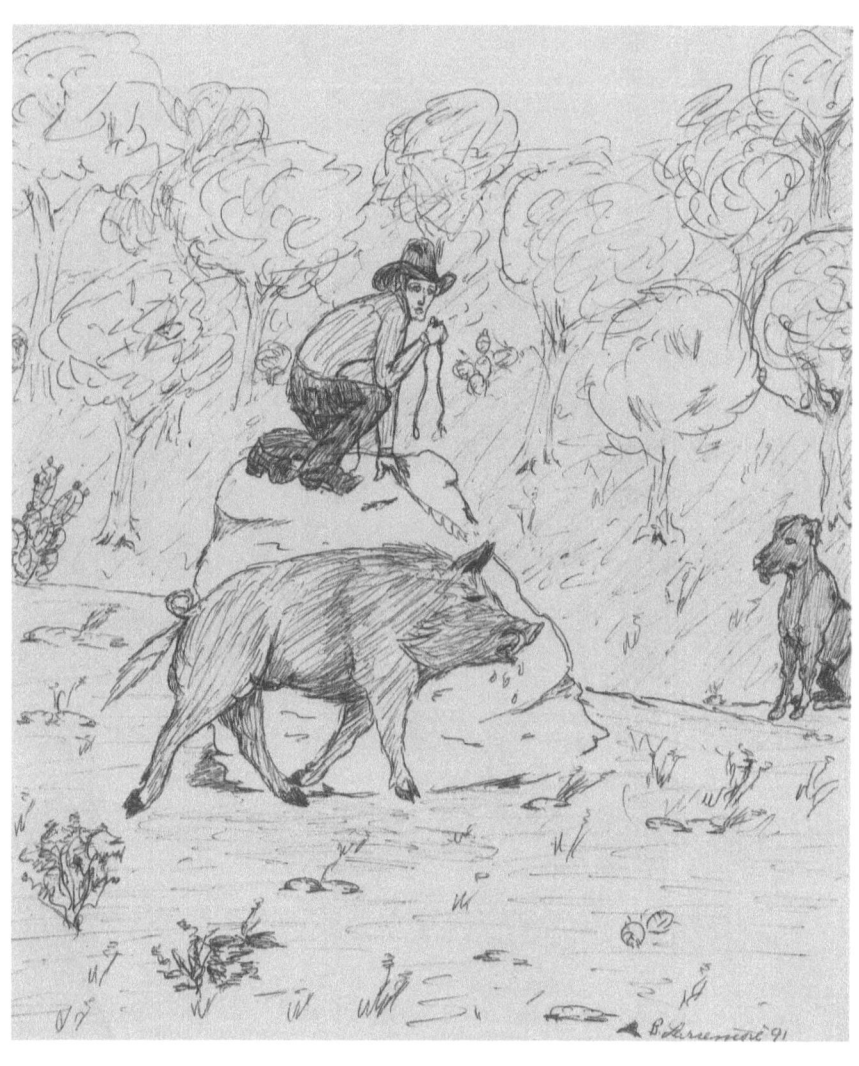

Dog, you're supposed to catch the pig!!

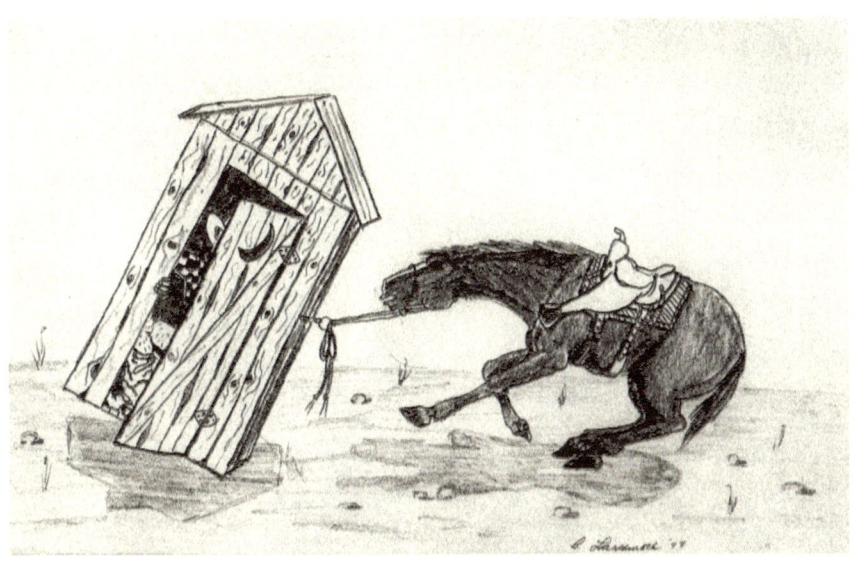

Whoa horse! That weren't no gunshot!

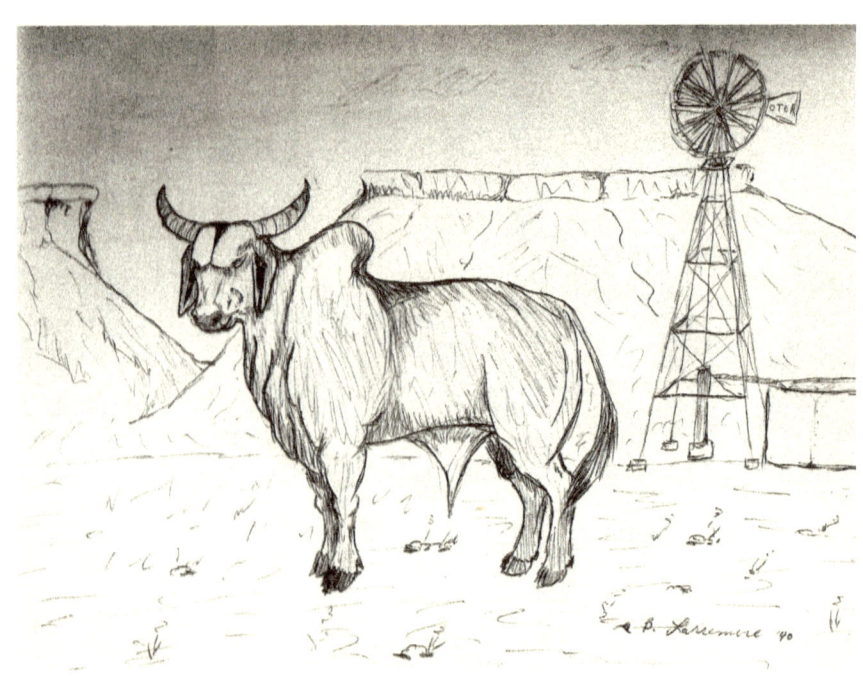

Look who's smiling now!

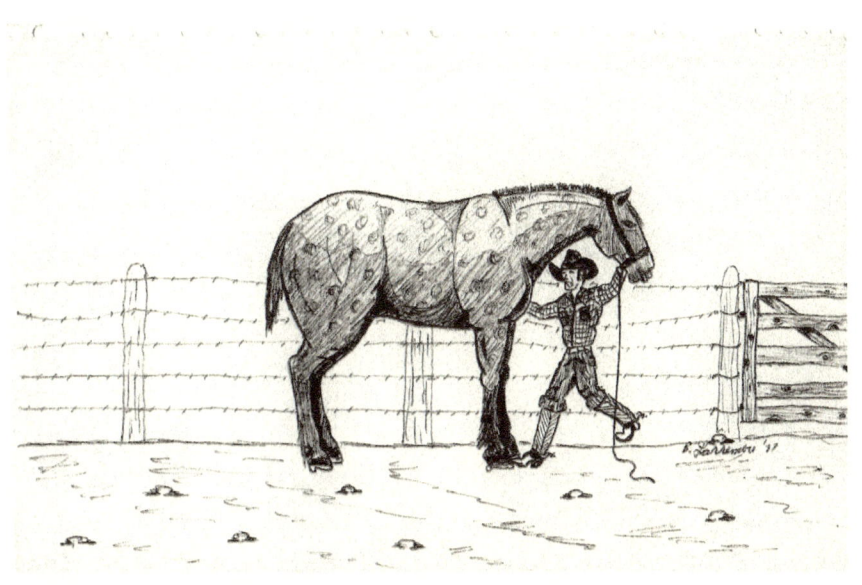

You wouldn't weight so much if you didn't have those horse
shoes on!

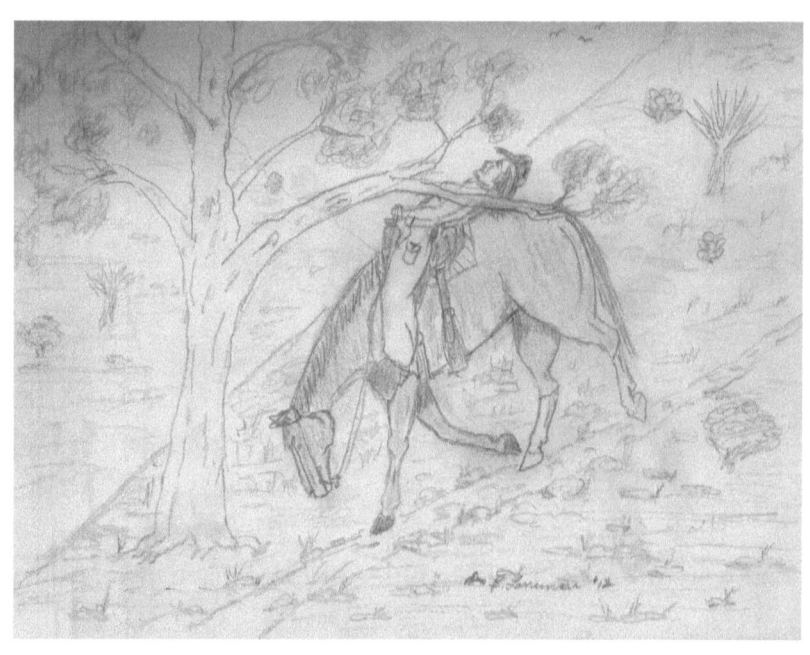

Jean, watch out for that tree!

LUTHER AND HIS SENSE OF HUMOR

My father-in-law, Luther, had a great sense of humor. He was always pulling stunts on people, stand back, and wait for the fun to begin. When Luther was in high school and living down at the ranch, he would find ways to poke fun at people. He always had another prank up his sleeve. One day he was doing some trapping and caught a bob cat. Bob cat furs weren't worth much in those days, so he figured he'd find something to do with that cat. After some doing he got the bob cat stuffed in an old suit case. He packed the suit case and the cat and gathered up some of his friends and drove out highway 90 going towards Marfa, Texas. He and his friends set the suit case along the highway and crawled up in some rocks where highway 90 goes into the mountains and they set up to watch what would happen.

Before too long, a big long black car came by. It slowed down and passed the suitcase then slowly turned around and made its way back toward the suitcase on the other side of the highway. The car turned around again, after it had passed the suitcase a second time, and started by it a third time. It was easing down the highway, the back door opened, and a long arm reached out and grabbed the suitcase and jerked it into the car. The car took off and about 100 yards down the highway, all the doors flew open. People started piling out, and they gave the car to the bob cat with the car still going about 30 to 40 miles an hour. Luther and his friends never did see their bob cat again and boogied back to town as fast as they could before they got caught.

PILE DRIVEN

Back in the late 70's, early 80's, Apache Adams was running cattle on Terlingua Ranch and the lower Big Bend of Texas when it was open range. Roddy Schoenfeldt, Sam Dove, Rod Devoll, Greg Locke, myself and several other people, were helping Apache gather cattle in that big old open country. We'd gotten them penned and were working calves. Apache was dragging calves by their back feet. Greg Locke was tailing and his partner, who was a Mexican man named Lalo, and spoke no English, was supposed to be jerking the rope. Lalo wouldn't get the rope, but would run around to the calves head instead. The calf would run around Greg and get him tangled up in the rope. Greg was telling Lalo in Spanish to stay back, pull on the rope and pull on it to throw the calf. Apache drug up about a 500 to 600 pound heifer, and Lalo ran around to the head, and the heifer ran around Greg and gave some slack in the rope; the rope caught right above Greg's spurs and then everything went tight.

When it went tight, Greg was jerked right straight upside down about six feet in the air, his boots went about 15 feet right straight up in the air, and Greg was pile driven right straight down on his head. Greg got up, pointed his finger at Lalo, and told him in Spanish, "you son of a b___, go get in the corner and don't come out!" Lalo went over into the corner, squatted there and was mumbling to himself. We got Greg back into his boots and went back to work. Directly, Lalo came out of that corner chattering just like a monkey. Apache, who was raised on the river across from Mexico, couldn't understand a word Lalo had said. Roddy had run a trading post on the river and he couldn't understand Lalo either. Finally, someone asked Rod if he understood what Lalo was talking about. Rod said, "I think what he said was, "don't point your finger at me when you call me a son of a b____!"" We all figured it was okay to call him a son of a b____, we just couldn't point our fingers at him if we were doing it.

RODDY AND ROCK

I believe it was the same works with Apache, and we had made a real long big circle, gathering cows. Roddy was riding a 3 or 4 year old mule out of a Triple A running mare that he called "Rock." It was about 3:00 or 4:00 in the evening and none of has had a drink since early that morning. We drove the cattle within about 200 or 300 yards of the VFW. Roddy quit the herd and rode over to the VFW and got him a beer. He came a jigging up on his mule sipping that beer and passed Rod and Sam. Roddy was telling them how good that beer was as he rode by. Apache was on the same side of the herd as they all were on and saw Rod look at Sam and Sam look and Rod and one of them flipped the end of a rope to the other one and Apache quickly moved to the other side of the herd. Roddy heard them coming, looked back and saw them coming with the rope stretched between them and threw that beer right straight up into the air as high as a man can throw a beer and went to gathering reins. He was too late.

That rope hit old Rock right under the tail. Rock left and outran both horses.

Mule races were popular at that time and Roddy took Rock to several mule races. As long as Roddy could break him out front, Rock never lost a race. Rock didn't want another rope up under his tail.

RODDY AND THE ROCK HEADER

Roddy called me to work cows off Elephant Mountain because he thought the cows were running out of water up on top. We rode to the top of the mountain and there was still plenty of grass left. Roddy said we should ride by an old rock header that might have water in and that we should check it out. Roddy hadn't been working at Elephant Mountain Ranch very long and didn't know how deep the water might be. It was bout 20 degrees and the wind was blowing about 40 to 50 miles an hour, and we didn't really want to have to try to drive those cattle off. Roddy decided he would ride through the water behind the rock header and see how deep it was. He rode in about 4 or 5 steps and him, horse, and all sunk plumb out of sight. The horse came up swimming carrying Roddy with him and came out the other side. Roddy, his teeth chattering, said, "there's enough water in here for these cows to stay up here 3 or 4 months." He pulled his leggings off to cover his shoulders to cut the wind and we hit for the house at a high trot..

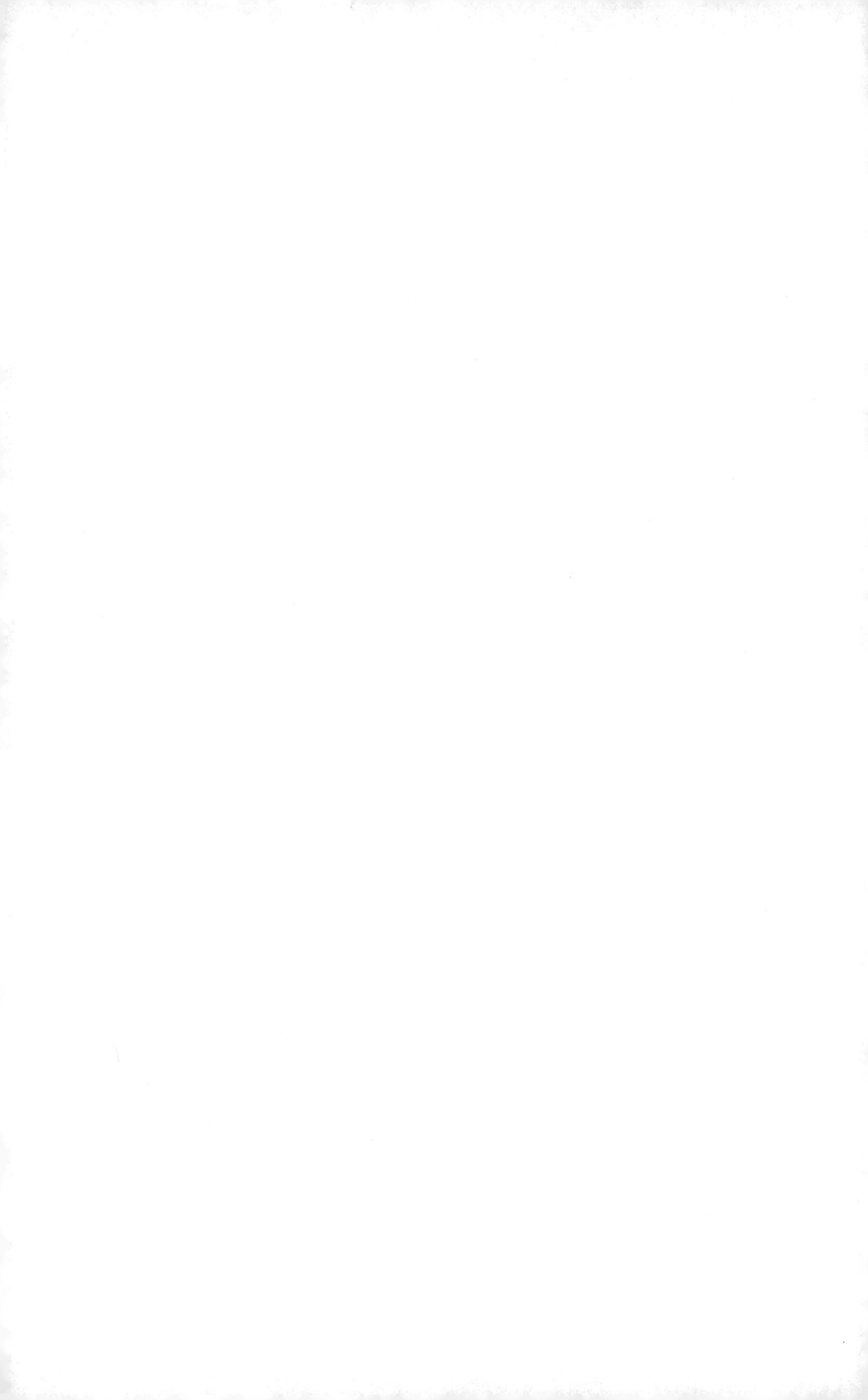

Apache and Pinto Canyon

Apache had leased Pinto Canyon in Presidio County, Texas and was needing some help gathering cattle. I told him that I probably couldn't get there till 10:00 or 11:00 that morning cause I had worked all night. He said that would be alright, just as long as I got there. I was able to get off work from the college earlier then I thought I would and got to Pinto Canyon 2 or 3 hours earlier than what I'd told Apache. I drove up and he came out of the horse pens. He said, "I sure am glad to see you." I told him "I'm glad to see you too, but why are you so glad to see me?" He said, "That old bay horse I got from Felix Valenzuela done throwed my saddle off 3 times and I really wasn't wanting to get on him till someone else was around." He wondered if I thought we ought to pull that old bay to the top of the mountain, or should we start him out at the bottom. I told him I thought we ought to start at the bottom of the mountain cause that horse couldn't buck near as hard going up that mountain as hard as he could going down it. Time we got to the top of the mountain that old bay was warmed up and never did buck.

JOY ADAMS TAKES A RIDE

We started out to gather down at Elephant Mountain and Apache's wife, Joy was with us. She was riding a real good horse named Leo. Apache was riding a bay colt with a heart branded on his left shoulder. We all mounted up and started to leave the pens. Apache's heart horse kept humping up and wanting to buck. Apache reached up and jabbed him up in the shoulders with both spurs and hollered, "You want to buck, buck!!" The horse throwed up his head and the hump went out of his back. Leo blew up on Joy and was bucking like a scalded dog in a circle. I was riding a good horse and riding in a circle trying to get to Leo's head to pull him up, but was bucking too fast for me to get there. Leo finally quit bucking and Joy said something to the effect of, "Apache, don't do that when I'm with you!" Apache said, "Well darling, I didn't think he'd buck, but you sure did make a pretty bronc ride!"

Gathering Remnants with Tommy Vaughn

Tommy Vaughn called me one day and asked me if I could bring my dogs and horses to help him gather remnant cattle off the Merriweather Ranch north of Alpine, Texas, for Sanford Devoll as Sanford had lost his lease. Tommy had 4 or 5 good Leopard/Mountain Cur dogs and I had about 4 Lacy and Leopard/Lacy cross dogs. Tommy had a pair of two-way radios and gave me one of them. He told me to call him on the radio if I struck the cattle. I headed east and he headed south. My dogs hit a cow trail and went to the cattle. They bayed 12 to 15 head of cows, calves, and yearlings down in a pretty good sized bowl ringed with boulders. I got on the handy-dandy radio and told Tommy I had the cattle east of him. In a little bit, Tommy came over the rim of that bowl at a dead run and was right in the middle of those cows before he knew it. He scattered cows all over the place. We both went to hollering at the dogs, the dogs circled the cows and we sat and held them up for a while. One old cow kept trying to break out and the dogs would bring her back. She finally decided she would stay with the bunch. We called our dogs back and finally started towards the pen. After 2 or 3 break-outs, we penned them. We took a break to get our wind and let the dogs and horses cool off and directly one old cow just flat-footed jumped the fence and took off. I asked Tommy if he wanted to try and go get her. Tommy said, "no it's been a long run. The dogs are too hot and the horses are too tired, and so am I." We never saw that cow again and never did figure out where she went.

TOMMY AND HIS FLAT LAND HORSE

Tommy took a sorrel streaked faced horse to ride and train. The horse came from the Fort Worth-Dallas area and belonged to Gerald Swindell. He was about 90 percent idiot and didn't know what a rock, tree, or cactus, was. We went to the top of Kokernot Mesa which is accessible only by horseback. Kokernot Mesa is about 600 feet from the valley floor and about 300 feet of it is talus slope and rock slide. The shortest way off the mountain was the steepest worst trail. One we jokingly call the "Snake Trail," cause it's not fit for a snake to crawl up. I don't believe in walking when I've got a good horse, but on this trail, I'll lead my horse to be able to give him a chance to stand up. We started off that trail and that horse of Tommy's had his head right straight up in the air. That horse would fall off the trail; Tommy would be holding him by the end of those 8 foot reins, and say, "you s.o.b., if you didn't have my saddle on you, I'd turn you loose." The horse fell off the trail three different times. Tommy led him all the way to the bottom. By the time we reached the bottom that horse had his head down almost between his legs, watching where he was going. Tommy said he didn't think that horse had enough sense to make a good horse; all he was fit for was a pack horse.

MILK COW IN THE NIGHT TRAP

I was working up at Sul Ross and trying to run the Larremore-Anderson Ranch, and I would try to keep a college kid down at the ranch to help me out. I had one kid who proclaimed himself to be a bull rider and bull fighter. He was married and decided he wanted a milk cow. I knew where there was a 2 year old bred Jersey heifer that had never been handled much. I told the boy I would try to get the heifer if he would break her to milk and milk her, because I didn't have the time to fool with her. He said that he would. I bought the little Jersey and brought her home. She probably didn't weigh 500 pounds. I hauled her to the ranch and unloaded her in the pen and set the gates down the alley to the chute. I told him to run the cow down the alley and put her in the chute.

He walked into the pen, the cow snuffed and charged him and the kid went over the fence. I told him, "I thought you were a bull fighter?" He said, "Yea, but that's a cow!"

I walked into the pens, waved my arms and hollered at her. She went down the alley and straight into the chute. After a little while, she had her calf. My helper would get her in the chute, milked her, and let the calf suck. After about a week, we started turning the heifer out in the night trap during the day. After about a week, she didn't come in one evening. The kid had a roping horse he was real proud of, and I told him to saddle up and go gather the milk cow. He rode off into the trap, and about an hour later he rode back up the house without the cow. He and his horse were both wet from the neck down, and he didn't have the rope on his saddle that he had ridden off with. I asked him what happened. He said, "I rode up next to the creek and that cow was bushed up next to the creek. I hollered at her, and she came out of the brush and knocked me and my horse into the creek. So, I just thought I'd rope her. When I did, I missed my dallies, and she's dragging my brand new rope all over that old nasty pasture." I told him to let me borrow his horse. I rode out in the pasture, found the little cow, hollered at her, and she headed for the pens at a high lope. That was the last time that little old Jersey heifer got milked.

JIM AND SORRELY

When Jim was 12 years-old, we were living in Corona, New Mexico. He decided he wanted to get a colt and break it. I went to the Roswell horse sale and bought a yearling sorrel colt with a white streak down his face for $200.00. I bought a fairly small yearling cause Jim wasn't going to be able to get on a very tall bronc. We went through the process of getting him broke and got him started without him bucking. Jim named him Sorrely. We moved to Marathon, Texas, and Jim started playing 7th grade football. Jim got a little lax about riding the colt. I kept telling him he better ride that colt. He'd say, "aw, he's gentle." Jim hadn't ridden that colt for about six weeks. One Saturday, Jim said he'd go out and ride that colt. Jim saddled up Sorrely and started to step on him. I told him, "Jim, I'd warm that colt up if I was you." He said, "aw, he's gentle." I told him, "yea, but it's thundering and lightening around here and he might not take that too well." Jim repeated, "aw, he's gentle." Sorrely took about

4 or 5 steps and blew up. The old colt could buck. He threw Jim up in the air with about 4 or 5 flips. The colt came down and started back up, and Jim was coming down face first. Jim's nose met the saddle horn. Jim got up, walked around behind the saddle shed. Ann, his mother, was sitting up on the fence. I was halfway up on the colt when I thought to myself, this won't do the boy or the colt any good. I said, "Jim, come here and get on him." Jim had on a white shirt and the whole front of that white shirt was covered in blood from a broken nose. His mamma slapped her hand over her mouth, took a real deep breath and didn't say a word.

I held the colt while Jim got on and told him to ease Sorrely around. Jim walked a good while, trotted a good while, and finally got Sorrely into a good lope. I told Jim to go on into the house and get cleaned up and get his nose bleed stopped and then to come on back out. I started warming up that colt and when Jim came back out that colt was white with lather. Jim went ahead and got back on him and rode him some more and said he thought Sorrely was ready to go outside. There was a section trap behind the horse pens. Jim started Sorrely around that section trap. I climbed up on the fence and finally on top of the saddle shed so I could keep them in sight. I climbed back down before they got back to the pen. When Jim rode up, I asked him how it had gone. Jim said, "old Sorrely tried to buck in that first corner down there, but I just whupped the crap out of him, then he behaved himself."

That colt got to where he'd do anything Jim asked him to do. When Sorrely was about 4 years old, we moved to a ranch north of Marathon. We were separating dry cows from cow and calf pairs. We missed one cow that had a calf and when the cow started bawling for her calf across the fence, I realized we needed to get her back into the pasture. Jim, Shawn Yadon and I went around her and tried to push her through the gate. She put a kink in her tail and headed straight away from the gate, right through our horses. I knew the old cow and she was pretty ringy. I stepped off and tightened my cinch up. Jim went right on around me and roped the cow. That cow jerked that saddle right up over the withers of that horse. Jim rode Sorrely up and turned him around, and that cow jerked that saddle nearly onto Sorrely's rump. Jim would turn the colt around and that cow would jerk the saddle the other way. This happened 7 or 8 times. Jim finally got the cow wound around a dagger about the time Shawn and I caught up. We caught the cow and tied her down. We went and got the truck and trailer and finally put her back to where she belonged.

Not too long after that, the 4H club was having a play day for the kids. Jim decided he wanted to take Sorrely to see what he would do. Sorrely had never seen the barrels, the poles, or the stake race. Between each event, Jim would take him around the barrels once, the poles once and the stake race once. He won two out of the three events and won second in one of them. That $200.00 colt in a hackamore was running against and beating some $8000.00 and $10,000.00 horses. Jim had done a heck of a job training him. When Sorrely was 9, Jim sold the horse to some folks out of Sierra Blanca and that colt raised their 3 daughters and took real good care of them.

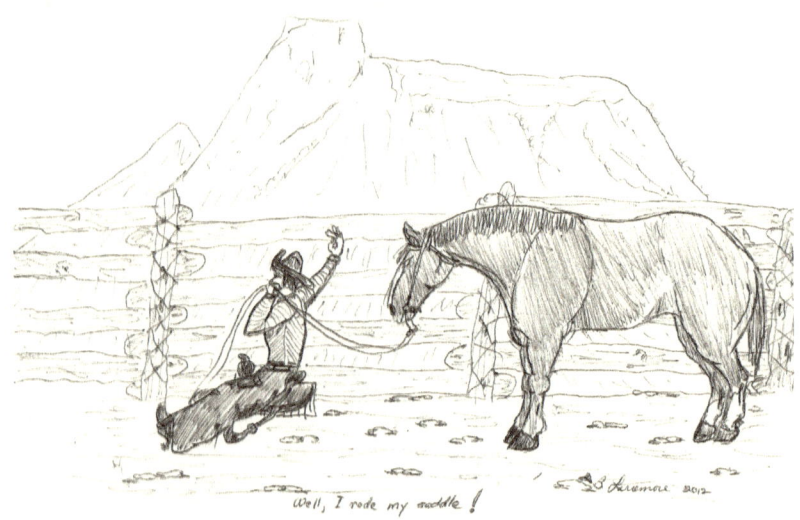

Well, I rode my saddle !

Don Coleman and the Plow Footed Horse

Don called me and asked me to come work cattle with him over at Cathedral Mountain south of Alpine. We all saddled up and were fixing to mount up. Don had a big plow-footed horse, by which I mean that it was a big draft horse like a Budweiser horse. When Don stepped on the horse; the horse blew up. The first thing Don knew he was sitting on the ground still in his saddle, still holding his reins. Don said, "I may not have ridden my horse, but I rode my saddle. Plumb to the ground."

ADOLF HONIG AND SMOKEY JACK

I was down in Llano visiting my brother Gary. He was indisposed with the stomach flu. Adolf Honig drove up and asked Jeanne, Gary's wife, if he wanted to go look at a horse. Jeanne told Adolf that Gary was sick and couldn't go anywhere right then. He turned around and looked at me and asked me if I wanted to go. I told him I'd always go look. I followed him over to his ranch and he caught a zebra stripped, smoky dun that weighed about 900 pounds, was 15.1 hands, and plumb covered up with ticks. Adolf said the horse was 5 years old. I had my saddle with me and saddled him up. I turned him around 2 or 3 times and stepped on him. I eased him around in a walk, slow lope, and a trot. He didn't want to handle very well, but he didn't blow up and buck me off. I came back, dismounted and asked Adolf what he'd have to have for the horse. He said he couldn't take less than $500.00. I told him the horse was awful green for a 5 year old and I didn't think I could give over $150.00.

Adolf said he might be able to take $400.00. I told him that I might be able to go up to $175.00. He said, well, maybe $300.00. I pulled out two $100.00 dollar bills and started rubbing them together. I said, "$200.00 is all the money I've got." Adolf said, "I can't take $200.00. I can't take $200.00. I can't take $200.00. Aw hell, I'll throw in the halter," as he was reaching for the money. He then told me the horse hadn't been ridden since he was a two year old because he had flipped over backwards with the man that was breaking him. Smokey Jack grew to be 16 hands and 1250 pounds. He made one of the best horses we ever had, and we kept him till he died at 22 years old.

HAIRLIP AND THE TOMATO SOUP

I had real bad ulcers for a long time, and sometimes it was real hard for me to eat anything except Dr. Pepper floats and soups. One day my mother-in-law, Tinny, made me some homemade Tomato soup, and it was as good as you ever flapped a lip over, for lunch. I went out and saddled one of my horses I called Hairlip. Hairlip came from south of Marfa and in the winter he was light yellow and in the summer was a light grey. He stood 16 hands, weighed about 1300 pouns, and was about 9 years old. He had a mustache on his upper lip so I just called him Hairlip. Hairlip was one of the toughest horses I'd ever ridden. No matter how much you rode him, he wouldn't tire out. After I got on Hairlip, we started up to check waters and riding pasture, and about a quarter of a mile away from the house that Tomato soup came up before I ever had a chance to get off the horse. Hairlip went to spinning away from that soup and he spun fast enough that he came back to it before it would hit the ground. He spun the other way and met it before it hit the ground, and I was still throwing up. All I could do was hang on to the saddle horn and puke. He spun back and forth about 5 or 6 times. I finally stopped throwing up, and he quit spinning. I sure was glad, cause I was about to lose my grip. I thought I would have painted him red, but he never got a drop on him. I had to wait a while for everything to settle down before I could ride on.

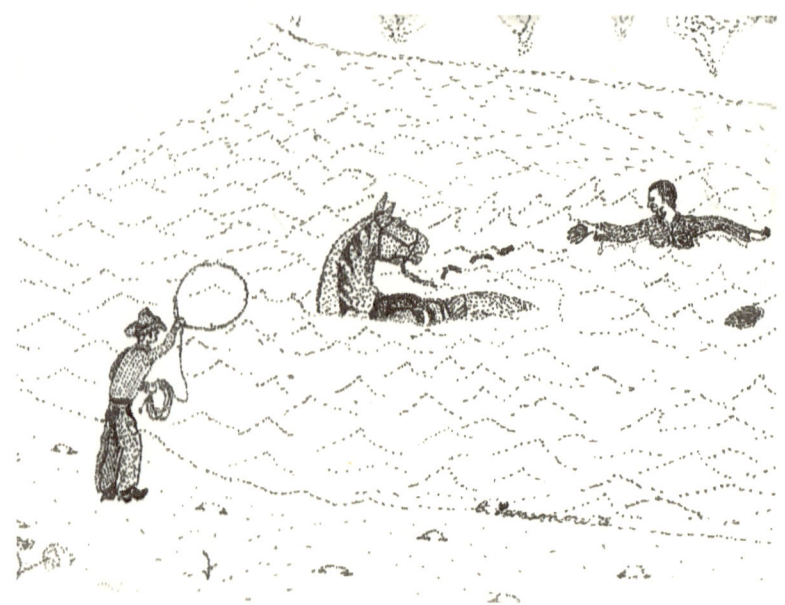

Rope my saddle

In 1966 I was breaking colts for Faith Cattle Company, south of Carrizo Springs, Texas, down in the brush country. Leonard Haynes was foreman, and Billy Ward worked with me snubbing my colts for me. Billy Ward would take over the colts after I got them pretty well started. It had been raining, and the creeks were running pretty good. Leonard told us to take a couple of those old colts and ride the fence. We were going to have to cross one pretty good creek, but Leonard said it had a pretty good rock bottom crossing. Billy said he knew where the crossing was. I was riding a roan colt and Billy was riding a red dun colt that he wanted to put in his string. We got to the crossing, and Billy told me to go on ahead. I told him I didn't know where the crossing was, and I'd follow him. He started across and apparently the crossing had washed out, or he'd missed it. They both sunk plumb out of sight. Billy came up swimming, and the colt came up floating without ever trying to swim. The colt has his head stuck up in the air and just went floating off down the creek. Billy headed toward the bank swimming with his boots and leggings on and hollering, "Catch my saddle, catch my saddle." We'd been roping some old nannies so the horses knew what a rope was. I caught the red dun around the neck, and the roan colt pulled him until the red dun scrapped bottom, where he got up. Billy and I both smoked, but all our cigarettes and matches were wet. He said that Leonard would be coming along the dirt road to the road crossing before long, and we could get some cigarettes. When Leonard came along, he said, "I thought you were supposed to be riding that fence." Billy explained the situation to him and asked him for some cigarettes. Leonard said, "Here's you some cigarettes. Ya'll might as well just go on back to the barn and dry out." We did so gladly cause we were wet, cold, and miserable.

BLAZE

My brother Gary was working for Harve Cogdell between Marfa and Alpine. Harve put Gary on a little blaze-faced, sorrel, stocking-legged 3 year-old that was out of a Prude mare and an Espy stud and not registered. Harve had Gary cutting cattle in an alley, but the little horse wasn't wanting to cut. Gary had to eat him pretty good with his spurs. The little horse blew up and crow-hopped about 4 jumps. About a month later, I was working on the Morrow Ranch between Alpine and Marfa. Harve had the little horse there, and I saw him and like the looks of the horse. Harve got to telling me that he was wanting to trade the little horse off cause he was getting too old to ride colts and the little horse had crow-hopped with my brother. We had a roan horse that was real gentle about 11 years old. I told Harve about him and he thought the roan horse would be about what he needed. I rode the colt, he road my horse, and we made the trade. I took the horse home and rode him. Riding across the pasture, I just had to peddle him all the time. We named him Blaze.

About the third time I rode him, I came in tired and give out from having to peddle him all day and told my wife Ann, that I was going to give her that horse and thought she'd like him because he was pretty lazy, and she ought to like him. She said she would take him. Awhile later I was up helping Don Coleman and Bill Fowler on the Merriwheather-Cathedral Mountain Ranch south of Alpine. There was a 2 year old heifer there that Bill wanted to cut out and asked me to rope her and drag her out. I told him there was no way that Blaze would pull that 800 pound 2 year old heifer out of there. Bill told me to go ahead and try him. I healed the heifer and Blaze just got down on his belly and drug that heifer out of the pen on her side. I said, "I didn't' think he'd do that!" Bill told me to go ahead and drag calves on him. Blaze never made a bobble. He kept me where I needed to be and he drug those calves like a 20 year old horse.

When I got home, I told Ann that I really didn't think she wanted that old horse, he was just too blooming lazy. She asked what he had done. I told her again, I thought he was just too lazy to get along with. She again asked what he had done. I had to break down and tell her what all the horse had done. I never did get him back.

About when Blaze was a 6 year old, Leanna started riding him. They were the same age. I've seen Leanna get off balance and start to fall off, and Blaze would step under her to keep her on. Ann or either one of my kids would get on that horse, and he would hit that little fox trot of his, and they would never have to touch him with a spur. I'd get on him, and I'd have to spur him all day if it was across the pasture, but if I ever pulled my rope down, I was horseback and never had to touch him with a spur. Leanna went to the 4H play days and rode him a lot and showed him. She never got in any hurry in any of the timed events, but he would win champion at halter, place first in the trial ride, and generally place 1st or 2nd in Western Pleasure nearly every time. The County Agent, Joe Winstead, would tell Ann and Leanna that he didn't know why the judges would place that old common grade horse over those good registered horses. He said it to where I heard it one day and I told him, "Joe, have you ever considered that old grade horse maybe isn't so common? He does everything that little girl asks him to do and is never going to hurt her and will always take care of her."

As I said, Leanna would take her time around the barrels, just lope and trot. At one play day, they had a calf roping for the high school boys. Carmen Henderson and his son, John D. were there, but John D. didn't have a horse. Leanna heard John D. tell his daddy that if he had a horse he'd get in that roping. She asked me if it would be alright if John D. could rope off of Blaze. I told John D. he was welcome to use Blaze to rope on if he wanted to rope. He said, "that old thing?" Carmen told him, "I'd listen to the man if I were you." I said, "you're going to have to wake—him up, cause he's used to packing Leanna around. You come out of that chute and over-under him with that rope, and he'll put you on that calf. You'd better be ready to throw that rope." All the other boys missed their calves. All John D. had to do was catch. John D. did what I told him to. Blaze looked back both sides when John D. over and undered him, and put John D. on that calf. John D. caught, got off, tied the calf, and won the roping. He walked up to Leanna and told her that was one of the best horses he had ever rode. She thought a lot of John D., and that sure did make her proud.

When Leanna was 17, she decided that Blaze needed to go to a little better home and take care of somebody else's kids. She sold him to Gage Holland for his granddaughters. We lost Leanna shortly after that. About a month later, Blaze was struck by lightening and killed. She is still riding him up in heaven today.

www.ingramcontent.com/pod-product-compliance
Lightning Source LLC
Chambersburg PA
CBHW020252290526
45784CB00003B/1217